# A Child in the Forest
## Winifred Foley

Winifred Foley became a professional writer at the age of sixty, when *A Child in the Forest* was first published in 1974. The remarkable success of the book, and of the Woman's Hour programmes on which it is based, initiated two further works of autobiography, *No Pipe Dreams for Father* (Futura, 1977) and *Back to the Forest* (Macdonald & Co., 1980).

Mr and Mrs Foley live in Gloucestershire, ten miles from the village of her childhood.

# A Child in the Forest

## Winifred Foley

ARIEL BOOKS
BRITISH BROADCASTING CORPORATION

Published by the British Broadcasting Corporation
35 Marylebone High Street, London WIM 4AA

First published 1974

This edition first published 1986

© Winifred Foley 1974

ISBN 0 563 20451 6

Typeset by Phoenix Photosetting, Chatham
Printed in Great Britain by Cox & Wyman Ltd, Reading

# Contents

## Dedication

To my parents, husband, four children, their
spouses, and the grandchildren, for all the
rewards I have garnered as daughter, wife,
mother, mother-in-law and granny.

# Introduction

If fair comment is to be observed, I cannot claim this book to be 'all my own work'.

That it progressed from its shabby beginnings of hand-written pages in dog-eared exercise books into stiff covers with a smart jacket and was launched on the public, is due to the efforts of many.

I was first scolded and cajoled into serious attempts at writing by my niece, Elizabeth Ann. I was also able to poach freely from my husband's superior vocabulary.

However, struggling would-be writers like me, unable to judge their own efforts, need more than a fair share of help and encouragement.

Two busy literary gentlemen – David Thomson of the BBC, and John Burnett, Professor of Social History at Brunel University – kindly read some early efforts, praised them, and advised me to persevere.

Fortunate struggler, how lucky for me that I submitted them to Pamela Howe, a talks producer in the BBC at Bristol. She became a would-be writer's fairy godmother.

First she had my scripts typed, and this tedious chore was cheerfully done by her secretary, Christine Wesnes, who heartened me still further by taking a lively friendly interest; then Pamela brought them to the notice of *Woman's Hour*. The Editor and the serials producer, Pat McLoughlin, bless them, agreed to let Pamela produce it as a *Woman's Hour* serial.

Before this could be done, the work needed skilled adaptation and an actress to read it. I couldn't have been luckier in having Virginia Browne-Wilkinson to make a radio serial out of the material, and June Barrie to give the highly praised readings.

Serials must have introductory music too. It was Pamela Howe's inspired idea to get a group of Forest children to sing *I'm Forever Blowing Bubbles* – a popular tune of the twenties I remembered my aunties singing when they came home on their brief holidays from service. Thanks to Miss Davies, the headmistress, and Mrs Davies, the music teacher, and a classroom of delightful children from Pillowell County Primary School, this 'theme music' proved so popular that some listeners asked for it to be made into a record! And indeed, how indebted I feel to so many sister listeners to *Woman's Hour*, who took the trouble to write letters of appreciation to the BBC and me.

When the BBC decided to publish the book, all the writings, plus the later story of my days in service, had to be edited and arranged; with unerring acumen and much friendly interest and advice, this has been done by Sheila Elkin.

To you all, my grateful thanks.

WINIFRED FOLEY

# Part I

# Our Village

At home I was 'our Poll' to my little sister and brother; 'my little wench' to Dad; 'a reglar little 'oman' sometimes, but often 'a slummocky little hussy' to my sorely tried Mam; to the ribald boys, 'Polish it behind the door', and to my best friend Gladys – just 'Poll'. Gladys was an only child, always clean and tidy, but she never turned up her nose at playing with me, even when the school nurse found lice in my hair, and my neck was covered in flea bites.

I was born in 1914, the fourth child of Charlie and Margaret Mason, but an elder brother and sister had died in infancy. Bess, called after Great-Aunt Lizzie, and four years older than I, was the eldest. When I came into the world, Dad was away in Wales because work was short in the Forest mines. A letter home to Mam included his 'love to my little fat Poll'. So Poll stuck, and though I was baptised Winifred in the village chapel, Poll I remained throughout my childhood.

When I was a child, the Forest of Dean was remote and self-contained. We were cut off from the world – from the rest of Gloucestershire by the Severn estuary, from Monmouthshire by the River Wye; and where our northernmost hills stopped, we stopped. A *Royal* Forest, it had been. Ten by twenty miles of secluded, hilly country; ancient woods of oak and fern; and among them small coal mines, small market towns, villages and farms. We were content to be a race apart, made up mostly of families who had lived in the Forest for generations, sharing the same handful of surnames, and speaking a dialect quite distinct from any other.

Few people visited the Forest of Dean. They thought us primitive, and looked down on us. I remember one visitor expressing pity for an elderly crippled man in our village, who'd never been outside the Forest. Looking slowly round, the old man said, 'Doosn't thee fret for I, me booy; I bain't tired o' round 'ere yet.' The Forest was that sort of place. As my father once said, 'Nobody wants to come 'ere if they can 'elp it; but once they do settle down, you'd atter shoot 'em to get 'em to muv.'

We children didn't think about whether we were isolated, of course, or about what the Forest was, or what its history had been. With our heads uncomplicated by lessons in botany or geology we took it for granted that hundreds of massive oak trees bordered our village, that the woods were full of ferns, that our fathers worked in coal mines. What was it to us that such a luxuriance of ferns was peculiar to oak forests? They were just there, to play and hide in. Some of us did know that the primeval forebears of the oaks we played under had formed the layers of coal far beneath us, where our dads crawled on their bellies to pick-axe it out; but we were too far away to feel the vibrations when a tunnel pit collapsed and somebody's dad or uncle, brother or grancher, wouldn't see the sunlight again.

Birds of a feather flock together, and in our village at that time the few feckless, filthy and friendly tended to live at one end; the prim, prudish and prosperous at the other. Between these two extremes lived a group of middling families, and this was where we fitted in. Here, in the centre of the village, lived a dozen or so families, not yet well off enough to move from their ancestral poverty, nor yet driven into complete squalor. The cottages – two up, two down, with a back-kitchen-cum-coal-house, had large gardens wrenched from the Forest under harsh 'Crown Rights' by industrious forefathers. Here were many children, but efforts were made to keep them clothed and fed, and even educated. Here gardens were cultivated and flower beds maintained. Pigs were kept and fowls. Most of the men were colliers, who showed a strong solidarity and fraternity. We were never anything but poor, but while we may not have been able to hold our noses in the air, we did try to keep our heads above water. We didn't carry pocket handkerchiefs or know what a dinner napkin was, but we were taught to show extra respect to the old and the handicapped. The dirt brought home from the pit, and on our boots, fought a constant battle with Mam's determination not to have her house 'turned into a turnpike road'.

Coal was no problem, except for the miners too old or too ill to work, for every working miner had an allowance of twelve hundredweight a month. The wonders of gas and electricity we only knew of second-hand from girls on holiday from service. Candles and paraffin lamps lit us up.

Often our home couldn't afford paraffin – or even, on occasion, a candle. Many's the time I've been sent around trying to borrow 'a stump o' candle'. Come to that, I was often sent for 'a pinch o' tay', 'a lick o' marge', 'a screw o' sugar', 'a sliver o' soap', or 'a snowl o' bread'. No one was ever optimistic enough to try to borrow money.

Each cottage garden was fenced with a dry-stone wall to keep out the sheep and pigs. Old iron bedsteads mostly served as garden gates. Any cottager who could afford it kept a pig; some were spare-time sheep-badgers, taking advantage of an ancient right to graze their sheep in certain areas of the surrounding forest. We children loved watching the dipping, shearing, and marking rituals, but only a hardy few could bear to watch the slaughter of a pig.

Pigs were regarded practically as neighbours. They had their own little stone dwellings alongside the cottages, and were christened with pretty names like Rosie, Sukey, or Ginny. Knots of men leaned over the pigs' gates to drool over the plump, succulent charmers in the pens. A weary, coal-grimed man would stop for a slap and a tickle with the pig before going indoors from work, answering her welcoming squeals and grunts with his own brand of piggy endearments. Shopkeepers would often refuse credit for family groceries, yet supply bran on tick for the pig; then they could claim half the pig at killing.

When the time came, poor Rosie's legs were tied and she was carried, squealing with terror, to the bench outside for the plunge of the butcher's knife. Mrs Protheroe was at the ready, with her great china washstand jug, to catch the gushing blood for her black puddings. Little girls stuck their fingers in their ears to deaden the pig's cries, and huddled together like wailing mourners. Boys war-danced round the blazing straw piled over the dead pig to burn off the bristles, and they waited to see who would catch the pig's bladder. When inflated, the bladder could be kicked around like a football.

Even when the grocer had had his half, the rest of Rosie still went a long way. The near neighbours all got a small share of the meat. The fat was rendered for lard (so tasty on bread with a sprinkle of salt). The big side-flitch was carefully salted on the slab in the back-kitchen. Later, when ready, it was hung on the living-room wall for the smoke to help keep it, as it was cut for use during the winter.

A flitch of bacon was considered the nicest decoration to have hanging on the wall, but the women were very fond, too, of religious texts to hang among the pictures. One new young wife artlessly hung two on the wall behind the double iron bedstead. One read 'I need Thee every hour', and the other 'Lord, give me strength'. It was years before she lived it down.

When I think of the 'slums' at the feckless end, the colour that comes to mind is grey. The children's skins were grimed grey with dirt; often a toddler's wash was from Mother's spittle on a corner of a filthy pinny rubbed around his protesting face. The interiors of the cottages were mostly grey, like the outsides. The ashdust from the grates settled in layers on the flagstone floors, on the home-made rag hearth-rugs and, mixing with the greasy cooking steam, finished curtains, walls and windows with a matching patina of drabness.

The feckless women 'dabbed out a bit o' washin'' when they felt like it, if they had the water; but all our water, apart from the rainwater, caught from the roofs in tubs, came from a well a quarter of a mile away, and one summer, when there was a drought, it dried to a trickle.

Hardly surprising that whatever colour curtains or clothes were to start with, they all ended on the clothes-line a uniform grey – at any rate, at the feckless end of the village.

Our mams, who never so much as had a dab of face powder to put on their noses in their lives, lugged the water from the well every day, but the washing was still done regularly every week.

When they got the water home, it was heated by a fire under the wash-copper, then poured over the dirty washing into a wooden tub; and the clothes and our mams were brought to a lather by the use of the unwieldy heavy wooden 'dolly'.

Clothes that today cannot be got rid of at a penny a bundle at the tail end of a jumble sale would have been thankfully washed and hung out with pride in those days.

Washing wasn't out on the line long; if the weather was wet, it must somehow be dried round the fire. Few had more than one change of clothing. In long wet spells, you might hear a woman call across the garden to her neighbour, 'I'll 'a to turn me britches an' shimmy this wik for we can't get near our vire for tryin' to dry the pit clothes out.'

Pit clothes took a lot of drying; men often worked in wet conditions underground, and would come to the surface soaked to the knees in mud. On dry days this caked up on the walk home and could be hit off with a stick; on rainy days, with walks up to three miles long, the men came home like 'drowned rats', as the saying was. When there were two or three men in a household working, the family were lucky to see the fire.

The village had no drains and no dustmen. The privy buckets were emptied into holes dug in the garden, slops were thrown between the cabbages; all other rubbish landed on the ashmix, sometimes only a handy throwing distance from the doorways.

The ashmix consisted mainly of buckets of ashes, with empty tins, broken china, and bottomless pails. It was a 'play centre' for bare-bottomed toddlers, who piddled into the empty tins and made mud pies with dirt and ash. Except in winter, children were often bare-bottomed till they were old enough for school. 'Bless his little arse' was a mother's commonest form of endearment.

Older girls pillaged the ashmix for tins, bottles, and bits of china to play 'houses' or 'shops'. Nearby stood a great chestnut tree, one alone among a forest of oak; each triangle of its exposed roots was a girl's territory. A bit of rusty iron bed lath, balanced on a stone with a cocoa lid on each end, made scales. We sold 'brown sugar' (sandy earth), 'boiled sweets' (little stones), and 'currants' (sheep droppings). In the long hot days of August we made cool tents from damp green fern that grew thick among the oak trees, or played helter-skelter down the slopes on old sacks.

Here we sat and lay, amusing ourselves lazily popping 'snompers'. We picked spikes of the beautiful pink foxgloves growing in profusion among the fern; then took off each flower, trapping the air with thumb and forefinger, and pushed the ends together till they'd explode with a pleasant little pop.

Tiring of this diversion, we would search for five small stones roughly the same size. These we would rattle about in a rusty tin until reasonably smooth, and then play 'jacks' with them. Town children call this 'five stones' but they buy them, neatly manufactured, from shops.

When we were very hungry and there was a chance of being called in for food, we would hint our presence to Mam by playing (near home) 'pigs, pigs, come to supper'. In this game, the other players turned their backs while a 'hidey girl' poked a piece of coloured china in a crack in a dry wall, between two marks. Whoever found it first became next 'hidey girl'. Often none of us could find it, not even the 'hidey girl'.

Life was wonderful except for one constant nagging irritation: hunger.

We knew that the wages our dads brought home from the pit were not enough to keep us out of debt, leave alone fill our bellies properly. We tried not to make matters worse by worrying our mothers for food. Everybody being in the same boat, we considered it good manners to refuse food offered by neighbours. The more the offer was pressed, the more vehemently we refused. Naturally enough, most of the stories we made up were filled with an abundance of delicious food.

But like other, less hungry, children we enjoyed ghost-stories too, and when the evenings grew shorter we scared the wits out of each other with them, until we were glad to run indoors before anything got us. It was nice to be indoors, safe from the cold. There was always a good fire. Most likely, on one side of it our Mam would be asleep with the baby on her lap, and on the other, old Great-Aunt with whom we lived. She was so crippled with arthritis, she just sat time away by the fire, and was smoked kipper-brown by the fumes.

If they were not at the pit, Dad and a couple of cronies would be arguing nineteen to the dozen about religion, politics, science, economics, or the fourth dimension. There they sat on their threadbare behinds putting the world in order. They sat the fire out, till the chill woke Mother up and she set about putting *her* house in order.

'Don't you men knew what time it is? Settin' there like a lot o' broody 'ens too idle to put a knob o' coal on the vire.'

She would plonk the baby on Father's lap, and rattle the poker between the bars, while the men, like scolded dogs with their tails between their legs, got out with as much dignity as they could muster.

Before she dozed off, Mam would have put our supper toast on the hob – just a few thick slices with the margarine spread only in the middle. No matter – toasted dry crust was delicious and we knew the art of chewing slowly to make it last. We kept very quiet so as not to wake Mam to supervise our bedtime wash. Into the little dark cold back-kitchen we sneaked, dipping our fingers into the well-used soapy water in a zinc bowl. We dampened the middle of our faces with our fingers; then we wiped off the loose dirt on a bit of towel hanging by on a nail. So up to the back-bedroom, three to a bed.

Then would come the best time of all. Our elder sister was our one-woman show. Her 'duet' rendering of *Madam will you walk* in high falsetto and deepest bass would give us hysterics. She could mime and mimic, and once did a 'Spanish' dance on the end of the bed, with a cracked soap dish for a castanet, turning it into a highly comical routine by scolding and smacking her elbows and knees for poking through the unmendable rents in the threadbare chemise of old Auntie's which she wore for a nightdress. Sometimes our laughter brought Mam away from the fireside, and she would threaten from the bottom of the stairs to 'larrup us' if we didn't keep quiet. Sometimes our sister said some magic words, and turned the patch of striped ticking on the quilt into a flying zebra. We all got on its back and flew over the rooftops to a much better place than Peter Pan found. Our sister never stinted us: everything we wanted was there. Jelly, custard and tinned pineapple to eat; a frilly pink silk dress with white shoes and socks for me; a real football and a little donkey for my young brother; dolls, marbles, proper skipping ropes with painted handles, and anything else we could think of.

'You be the best liar in the world, Bess,' we bragged. But our bellies rumbled.

As I dozed off to sleep in the warm safety of our shared bed, I listened to the plaintive wind in the forest trees which seemed to me to be the sighs of all the people that had died in our village, who wanted to come back to the Forest instead of going to heaven.

# Dad

Mam was the light sleeper in our family of slug-a-beds. She acted as alarm-clock to get Dad out of the house by five in the morning, for early pit shift. It meant her getting up at a quarter past four, to light the fire and make his tea and toast. Surplus tea was allowed to get cold; then, unsweetened and unmilked, it was put in a bottle. This, with 'a snowl o' bread' and 'a marsel o' cheese', was standard diet for all the miners in our village. The bread and cheese was put in a butty tin, so the underground rats wouldn't eat it.

To us children our Dad was the fount of wisdom, kindliness and honour. Whenever we wanted his attention he became a child among us – slow, dreamy and always understanding. He never minded being woken up at any odd hour to help with a fretful baby, or to nurse a sick child. Once, when I had earache in the small hours, he took me, sobbing with pain, downstairs; he made up a good fire, warmed a brick in the oven to hold up to my head to try and ease the pain, cuddled me on his lap and tried to distract me with the tales of Brer Rabbit, all to no avail. His blackened, beloved old pipe, charred with the residue of strong tobacco, was the balm and cure for all his own pains, and at last in desperation, he gave it to me.

'There, my wench, thee have a few puffs o' feyther's bacca – that'll take the pain away.'

And so it must have, for I awoke in bed, late the next morning, with my earache gone.

If he had a fault, it was the spending of sixpence on a book while his ragged shirt-tails were hanging through the ragged patches of his moleskin trousers. He loved to discuss his reading with his cronies. The fireside talk we overheard between them was full of H. G. Wells, Einstein, God, Darwin, Shaw and Lenin.

The men were all well read. With a sweep of a pit-grimed fist they dismissed bogus religious cant – and, equally, the cult of material wealth acquired for its own sake. They filled the world's belly with its properly distributed abundance, and the world's soul with the beauty of man's and nature's genius.

Concerts in our village were rare, but once when Dad had been working in South Wales, he'd gone to hear some classical music played, and had found it a profound experience. And when he heard that a violinist and his accompanist were to give a concert in our chapel, he was full of anticipation.

The chapel was packed. When the violinist began to tune up his instrument, the hobbledehoys standing together at the back sniggered, and called out who was pulling the cat's tail.

I was flabbergasted when Dad, the most kindly and tolerant of men, went to the back of the chapel and, quietly but firmly, told them to behave or get out.

In my eyes, Dad could do no wrong; but, earthbound little pleb that I was, I too thought the music sounded like cats on the roof. I looked for distraction in the nimble acrobatics of the pianist's fingers. Then I studied her face and peculiar hair style, then down towards her feet. 'Oh, my gawd, 'ers showing 'er combs!' I thought. Above her high, laced boots, the like of which I had never seen before, showed a three-inch band of light grey ribbed wool.

I turned to draw Dad's attention to this shocking exposure; but I could tell by his face that, though his body sat beside me, his spirit was far away.

As soon as the clapping started I leaned over the back of him to my sister on his other side, and drew her attention to my discovery. She sighed and gave me one of her 'whatever shall we do with her' looks. 'You sawney hap'orth! That bain't 'er combs a-showin', that be the top of them woolly stockings 'ers a-wearin' inside they boots!'

'Was it a good concert, Dad?' I asked him, as we walked home.

'Beautiful, my wench, beautiful. I only wish we 'ad some vittles in the 'ouse. I shoulda' liked to 'ave exed 'em up for a bite o' supper.'

Dad was a very polite man, the sort to put himself out to listen to the King if he'd come up by our gate, just the same as he put himself out to listen to poor old George the simpleton. Dad was the only person who could 'talk' to George's deaf and dumb wife. As a girl she'd been sent away to learn the deaf and dumb sign-language, but this still left her with not a soul to talk to, until Dad sent away for a book on the subject and taught himself.

It was fascinating to watch the pantomime of their gestures, and to see the remarkable change that came over Liza Baa, as we called her. Her face lit up, and she would laugh and look like a young girl. She was as thin as a rake, for simple George came at the end of the job queues, and like all the other women Liza gave the lion's share of the food to her husband.

When funds permitted us to buy the corn, Mam kept a few fowls, but Liza had only one old hen, and that was a pet, treated as one of the family. People said the old hen spent the night perched on their iron bedstead. That wasn't true, but it did go in and out of the house for any crumbs it could find under her table – or on it. Never having heard the human voice, nor what words sounded like, Liza relieved her emotions by a sort of moaning and cackling. That old hen used to scratch and peck round Liza's skirts, cackling back in an answering sort of way. They thought a lot of each other.

When Dad got pneumonia Liza came to see him. After a few days in bed he'd struggled downstairs to ease Mam's lot in attending him, and he was sitting grey-faced and hollow-eyed by the fire when Liza came in carrying a dish. The news of his illness had got through to her slowly. Now, in her hands, as clawlike as the old hen's feet swimming in the broth, was her sacrifice, to speed Dad's convalescence – her old hen. She put the dish on the table. Dad looked at the skinny stewed bird, and then at the beautiful kindness in her face. He had to bend down to do up his shoelaces, and when he looked up he could only nod his thanks. He'd been struck dumb, too.

That illness, we always believed, came from the conditions in which he worked when he was forced to go to a pit three miles from home. He was sacked from the pit near the village after the owner heard of his radical views and told the manager to get rid of him. The walk to the new pit wasn't too bad – it was downhill most of the way – but it was a hard grind home for an exhausted man at the end of a long shift. Mam put a stop to our usual practice of running to meet him for pick-a-backs up the garden path; but to reassure us that all was well Dad would do a little clog dance at the door in his heavy pit boots. Sometimes, as a bonus, just to show us 'yore feyther hen't a old mon yet', he would put the top of his head on the table, a hand each side, and slowly stand on his head. Muddied, streaked with coal-dust and rain, tattered and tired, he brought his radiance in with him. All was well when Dad came home.

Sometimes, on Sunday evenings, Mam went to chapel and left Dad to mind us. The lovely fire she built up before she left would easily lull him, as well as old Auntie, to sleep if we let it. Once, when he had only my brother and me to mind, we did let it. Then we set to work on Dad's hair. Only the fringe was long enough to do anything with; and not much with that, until we had the wonderful idea of putting a bit of treacle on it.

We had, at the time, a supply of brimstone and treacle for blood purification kept in the cupboard by the fire. We sneakily dipped a moistened finger in the tin, and rubbed what we didn't lick off on to Dad's fringe. Then we made it into a myriad tiny plaits, and tied these into knots, a feat of some dexterity.

By then we decided it was time Dad amused *us*. Usually, the first thing Dad did when he woke up was to make sure his beloved old pipe was on or near him. But on this occasion he put his hand to the top of his head, rose slowly, and went over to look in the little mirror hanging by the door.

'You young varmints! You've turned your old feyther into a bloody 'Ottentot. Whatevera' you bin a-puttin' on my yud?'

Although we helped Dad to wash off the treacle, and laboriously undid the knotted plaits, he still had a regular coxcomb of hair, that wouldn't comb down flat. 'I'll see you two buggers don't ketch I nappin' agyun.' Dad never growled, but he had a try.

Taking a piece of chalk from his pocket, he turned the wooden chairs we weren't sitting on upside down. 'Now, then, you pair o' bright sparks, what be these, then?' and he drew with his chalk, on the underside of the chair seats, his versions of some tropical animals.

We got so engrossed with this activity that Dad heard Mam saying goodnight to Granny only just in time. 'Look out! 'Ere be your Mam a-comin'!' In two shakes of a lamb's tail, Dad had put the chairs back upright, and we were sitting in innocent idleness round the fire when Mam came in.

Before leaving for chapel, Mam always left the house as spick and span as she could. After tea, she would put old Auntie's red plush cloth on the table, trim the wick of the lamp, fill its blue china bowl with paraffin, and place it in the middle of the table.

This grand, plush table-cloth had once had bobbles dangling all round the border; but in winter, during our toddler stage, the space under the table had been our 'play area', and most of the bobbles had proved irresistible to our meddling little fingers. But it was still a proud possession.

One evening, as soon as Mam had gone, Dad told us to sit up round the table. Then he went into the back-kitchen and came out with something he called an 'oojah-board'. It was roughly heart-shaped, had a sharpened piece of pencil fixed to the underside at the front, and moved easily on some small castor arrangement. We had known for the past week that Dad had been whittling away at something for us.

Next he smoothed down a big piece of brown paper across one end of the table. 'Now,' he said to us, 'one at a time, shut your eyes, and put your hand on thic oojah-board, an' just let'n vind 'is way about on thic piece o' paper.'

The ouija-board moved with practically no help at all. After a count of ten, we could open our eyes to read the 'message' it had written. But we could make nothing of our squiggles.

'Trouble is,' said Dad, 'thic bit o' 'ood I made'n from is mahogany, an' thic bloody board's a-writin' in jungle language. 'Ere, let I 'ave a goo, I'll see if I can persuade'n to write a bit in English.'

Dad screwed his eyes up very tight, and seemed to go into a trance of concentration. Then, suddenly, apparently of its own free will, the ouija-board began to write – not all that plain, but quite legibly: *Look behind the soap dish.* We fell over each other rushing into the unlit back-kitchen to feel behind the soap dish. Sure enough, something was there – a round piece of glass, with a metal rim on it, and a handle.

We were dumbstruck, and even more so, when Dad said that upon his soul, if it weren't a magic glass! Sure enough, when he put the glass over the hairs on his forearm and told us to look through it, his arm looked like a cratered, miniature jungle.

Every now and again, old Auntie surfaced to wakefulness to ask us, 'what's goin' on', or 'what be you up to now?'

We were up to looking for tiny objects to put under the magic glass. It took us out by the door to pluck a leaf left here and there on the roses, and to look by candle-light in the garden-wall for little slugs or mosses.

We gathered quite a variety of objects to spread over the best plush cloth. Time was forgotten, and our excited chatter drowned Mam's homecoming footsteps in the yard. The table was a shambles.

'Well! I can't turn me back on you lot for vive minutes afore you've turned the place into a regular menagerie!'

'What's a menagerie, Dad?' I asked.

'A zoo, I think,' said Dad.

'Yus, an' you be bloody well right,' said Mam, gathering up the plush cloth to shake its contents on to the garden.

Mam was an energetic type, and loved a bit of bustle to things: tables must be scrubbed till you could see the grain of the wood, fire-irons polished till you could see your face in them, rag mats shaken till the dust flew, and husbands who sat still too long hustled into some sort of activity.

'I can't see 'ow you're ever goin' to learn anything wi' your yud always stuck in a book,' was a frequent scold of Mam's. Brought reluctantly back to earth from the pages of *Erewhon* one day, Dad scratched his head and observed with impartial dignity to Mam, 'Mother, 'tis a great pity thee 'asn't got my brains, or I 'asn't got thy energy, then one on us coulda' come to summat.'

However, like all of her sex, Mam had her illogical moments. One Saturday evening, she told my brother and me that, as Dad and old Auntie would mind the two little ones, we could go to Cinderford with her to get some shopping.

This had happened one or twice before, and we knew it meant a treat for us. In the tiny market place, lit with naphtha flares, was a long table covered with white oilcloth, and flanked by wooden benches, where faggots or peas (or both to the rich) were served. The stall-owner was a stout, homely-looking matron, with a white starched pinny over her black blouse and skirt. Perhaps to give her round, motherly face a touch of dignity, and a 'no good to ask for tick' severity, she topped it with a man's cloth cap.

Spaced at strategic intervals on the long table were bottles of vinegar, and pepper and salt pots. The delicious aroma those faggots and peas sent out to the entrance would stop us in our tracks like kids in the Bisto advertisement petrified on the hoardings.

If she couldn't stretch things to have a penn'orth herself, Mam would take my brother and me to the table, order a penny dish of peas between us, 'two spoons please', and would leave us while she looked for food bargains.

The thought of those peas turned us into a willing little pair of carrier mules, better than a bag of carrots could work on the real thing. Mam never mentioned the peas, but they hung in our minds' eye all along the mile-and-a-half short cut through the Forest.

Dear Mam, she was one of the world's frustrated spenders, and would peer into every shop, with her short-sighted eyes, 'buying' all sorts for everyone.

One of her favourite shops was a junk shop at the bottom of the High Street. Sometimes there was a pretty vase or picture that she would take in her mind's eye, and place in a variety of positions to make her own home prettier. Her sighs gave me the clue to her thoughts.

There was quite a hint of excitement in her voice that Saturday, when she asked me to read out the titles of four enormous dusty, important-looking books in the window.

'*The Circle of the Sciences*,' I told her.

'Goo in, and ex 'ow much they be,' she told me.

"Alf-a-crown,' I had to tell her, surprised by such an odd request coming from Mam.

We always knew when Mam had a nice secret, although we didn't always find out what the secret was. We sensed, sometimes, that it was something she shared only with Dad. We knew because of the way she would purse her mouth up, and try to control her joy with little twitchings of her lips. I noticed it was happening as we walked on up the street. She also opened her purse, took the contents into her hand, and did a lot of thinking.

We were thinking hard, too, of the market and the faggot and pea stall, and could hardly persuade our reluctant legs to walk past it, as Mam carried on without apparently noticing the place.

Without batting an eyelid, she told such a tale of woe to the butcher that he knocked down the price of a big cow's heart to one-and-six. Mam came out looking well pleased with herself. Then down to the grocer's for flour, sugar, some tea, and very little else.

We cut round a place called the Triangle, back into the High Street, where we didn't have to pass the market. I squeezed my little brother's hand in sympathy.

There was a cake shop a bit further down. Mam looked in her purse again. "Ere you be,' she said to me, 'goo in and get a cake for you and Charlie to share.'

First we stared at the delectable array in the window, comparing size with exotic fancy trimmings, and mutually agreed that a cream slice would be the best buy. Mam broke it carefully in half between us.

Our faith in Mam, human nature, and the delicious wonders of life, returned. Mam hadn't even asked us to help her carry anything; one of the two straw frails she had brought was still empty. Well, it was till we got to the junk shop.

Then, full of pride, gracious as royalty ordering from Harrods, Mam went in and bought those four huge books for Dad. You could have knocked me over with the dust on them!

Mam put two of the books in the bottom of the frail with the shopping, and put the other two in the empty frail so that my brother and I could carry them, holding a handle each.

None of us had much fat to bring us out in a sweat, but what a huff and a puff we were in, and how our arms and legs ached. Had we been carrying those books for anyone else, Mam would have had a mutiny on her hands.

There was a lovely fire in the grate, and an air of expectancy indoors. Mam always tried to come home from such expeditions with something extra for supper.

'Kettle's a-boilin',' said old Auntie, and took the baby off Dad for him to wet the tea.

One by one, Mam heaved the books on to the table.

'They be for you, Dad. 'Alf-a-crown they was!' As usual I was precociously quick off the mark with any information.

Dad's mouth fell quite open, as he looked at those books with an expression that was a mixture of awe and bewilderment. No wonder! It was enough to make him awe-struck, Mam spending half-a-crown on books! His bewilderment was equally justified. Who could want books on science so out-of-date that the knowledge had become practically useless?

That was information to guard from her at all costs. Aware of Mam's scrutiny, he handled those books with as much reverence as if they'd come straight from the tomb of Tutankhamun. Then he looked up at her. 'Well *done*, Shuky,' he said, using his pet nickname for her. And the love in his eyes said volumes more than his words.

Mam was a generous-hearted woman. Possessions were easily procured from her with the wheedling tongue and covetous eye; but when she died, in her eightieth year, Father's books still had pride of place on the shelves in the alcove by her cottage fireplace.

# Mam

I don't know how our Mam ever managed to keep five of us fed and clothed – let alone herself and our Dad and Great-Aunt Lizzie, whom we lived with. Right from the beginning of our lives we children understood that we couldn't expect to have as much as we wanted of anything, and must never ask.

Mam was all but defeated by the problem of keeping her brood clothed. She was thankful for any garment that anyone would give her for us, regardless of fit or suitability. I kept a piece of string permanently round my middle to hold up the odd assortment of drawers I had to wear. The boys at school used to chant:

Sing, sing
What shall I sing?
Poll Mason's britches
Be tied up with string!

A stout middle-aged neighbour once produced a pair of her faded blue fleecy-lined bloomers for me. My piece of string kept them up, more or less, but the crutch came down to my knees, the bottoms almost to my ankles. 'Thee'st look like one o' they sultanas from a harem,' said my elder sister, Bess. I crept unwillingly to school, well behind everyone else. Before I got there I hid in the ferns, took off the bloomers, and chewed a hole each side of the waist. I put my arms through the holes, and wore them like a pair of combinations.

Another of my most memorable outfits was a frock that Mam once made me by sewing up a leg-of-mutton style lady's costume coat. It had shoulders as wide as a guardsman's, and plenty of braid trimming. It was most unfortunate that, on the morning I was to wear this to school for the first time, one of my aunts, who was in service, sent me a parcel of ribbon pieces. I had a passion for beads and ribbons, and forgot the misery of having to wear that terrible frock in the delight of all this treasure. I begged Mam to let me take the whole lot to school, and rather to my surprise, my sister joined in. I should have suspected her droll sense of humour, but as usual I didn't.

'Let me do thee up like Mary Pickford,' she said.

I had a short, pudding-basin haircut, a snub nose, a mouth that the kindly would describe as generous, a pair of unremarkable small blue eyes, and a trusting belief in Bess's genius.

On the way to school we kept well behind everyone else, then stopped for her to transform me. Somehow she managed to tie round my head, in loops and bows and streamers, every bit of that ribbon.

'My Gawd!' she said, almost overcome by the results of her efforts. 'I reckon thee'st do look better'n Mary Pickford – more like a fairy queen. Dance round thic tree so I can see how thee'st look when they ribbons do flare out.'

As she watched me dance, she suddenly doubled up with an attack of collywobbles, hardly able to speak for the pain, and decided to go back home instead of to school. Smirking, dreamy full of self-satisfaction, I carried on. One and a half hours late, I pushed open my classroom door, confident that I would create a sensation.

I did. The class teacher stared as though something obscene had crawled up through the floorboards. The titters of the class broke into roars of derision. Why, I thought despairingly, hadn't it been I instead of Bess who was struck down with the collywobbles? She always seemed the lucky one.

Clothing us was the worst thing, but feeding us was quite bad enough. The best effort Mam ever made in this direction nearly failed, for reasons which I suppose were foreseeable.

Someone whose sow produced a litter gave her the runt. Its chances of survival appeared to be very small, but Mam hand-reared it to a fat pink old softie that came running like a child at her call. Nancy would rub her snout against Mam's apron in the intervals of slurping up the contents of the wooden trough Dad had made her. The friendly cadenza of her grunting was so expressive, Mam reckoned she could talk, and sat on the empty up-turned bucket by the pig's-cot door to fuss and spoil her for a bit, no matter how busy she was. If anybody left the garden gate open, Nancy came waddling up the path, expecting to come indoors for a neighbourly social half-hour, and sniffled dejectedly when Mam smacked her behind all the way back to the gate.

Poor Mam! She saved Nancy's bacon as long as she could, but she'd no answer when Auntie scolded her: 'Thy young 'uns'll be lucky to 'ave 'er trotters to yut! If thee doosn't get the butcher to 'er soon, thee'la margaged'n all away.'

Mam had put one of Nancy's hocks 'in hock' to the grocer, towards payment for the bran, and the neighbours who'd given her their potato peelings were to have pieces. The butcher's services *had* to be ordered. For once I was speedy out of bed and off to school.

Mam was more courageous. It was she who cut the dried fern for the pyre to singe the bristles off Nancy, and she who filled the copper with water for scalding the singed offering. Mam made the sacrifice and did most of the work, but when it came to eating her plate of pig's fry, she felt the call to go down to the privy. Even Dad admitted ruefully that 'yuttin our Nancy nearly made us into cannibals'.

One Saturday afternoon in November we sensed that Mam was in a particularly good humour. Her mouth kept twitching at the corners as though it'd break into a proper smile if she wasn't careful. About four o'clock she pulled up her wrinkled lisle stockings, polished over the cracks of her only pair of down-trodden shoes, removed her sacking apron, put on her going-out costume coat, and announced that she was going shopping. Shops closed late in those days, and there were bargains to be had of meat and fish on the point of going off, and cheese too hard to stand another weekend in the shops.

Then she gave us our orders.

My elder sister was put in charge of the baby and making up the fire. After I had fetched in kindling wood, I was to spread a piece of newspaper on the scrubbed top table and clean our odds and ends of cutlery with powdered brick dust. I was also to help keep an eye on my younger brother and sister.

Then with dire warnings of what we should feel on our arses if we didn't obey these instructions, Mam made a sugar teat for the baby, took two straw frail bags, and was off.

The sugar teat was a couple of spoonfuls of sugar tied in a bit of rag and moistened by dipping into the kettle on the hob. The baby went to sleep before she'd sucked it down to the rag, so our elder sister, Bess, gave our little sister a suck on it, and promised my little brother and me could have one too if we would go and meet Mam when it got dark.

But first we must get the kindling. We didn't know the luxuries of topcoats or gloves, so I tied a couple of old woollen scarves from the nail behind the door round my little brother, and we went happily kicking among the autumn leaves for twigs and bits of fallen branches, breaking them into small lengths to go into the oven at the side of the big black-leaded grate to dry. Our dad got the miners' free allowance of coal so we always had a good fire.

I hated cleaning the cutlery and before starting arranged the forks and spoons into a row of 'piano keys'. On these I played my own tunes, singing an accompaniment of such excruciating tunelessness that my concert was brought to a sudden close by a clout round the ear from my sister.

It was almost a two-mile walk to the little mining town through the short cuts in the woods, and for us, in the dark, a much longer walk round by the main road along the edges of the Forest. Bess stuck a stump of candle in the bottom of a jam jar, and with thumping hearts my little brother and I set off, he holding the jam jar to keep his hands warm.

Almost all the trees in the forest were huge oaks – big enough for two witches to hide behind – but about half-way along the woodland path to the main road was a fine chestnut tree, and the weird hooting of a night owl seemed to come from its branches. My little brother knew as well as I that they pecked your eyes out in the dark. Taking the jam jar from him, I told him to keep his eyes shut, then the owl wouldn't be able to see him – walking myself with one eye open at a time, so as not to be wholly blinded at one fell swoop. The candle flame was flickering in a pool of melted grease, almost at the end of its wick; my courage had almost given out too.

'Me boot's undone,' I lied, and bent down, fumbling, to gain time, trying to hide my mounting terror of the chestnut tree.

Just then Mam's chesty cough heralded her approach.

''Oo be there?' she called, noticing our little glimmering light.

'It only be me!' I was now brave as a lion. With Mam about, the witches and ogres would fly for their lives. Even Dad, who wasn't afraid of the dark or thunder and lightning, melted into thin air a bit quick when Mam got her dander up.

'Well done,' said Mam. 'I could do wi' a bit o' 'elp wi' these frails. They be feelin' a bit 'eavy now.'

*That* was a good omen!

You never knew with Mam. There were times when she had come home with a bag of broken biscuits, or a comic, or better still with a bag of toffee pieces that had given us hours of glorious chewings.

When we got in, we found that Bess had chucked plenty of coal on the fire, but it took a few deft pokings between the bottom bars by Mam to send it into glorious flames, licking at the black flue. The baby whimpered miserably with hunger, despite Bess's desperate jiggings.

''Er'll 'a' to wait a few more minutes,' gasped Mam, wetting a pot of tea from the big cast-iron black kettle on one of the hobs. She put a lump of fat in a frying pan on the fire, then took some liver from one of the frails. She suckled the baby and drank her tea with one hand, turning the frizzling pieces of liver and adding flour and water, salt and pepper, with the other, till the liver bubbled in a pan of thick brown gravy. Liver for supper! We sat small and quiet, trying to be scarcer than we were, lest by some movement we should destroy or hinder the chance of the feast to come.

The baby, already worn out with her hungry crying, soon went to sleep at the breast. Mam put her down carefully in a chair and dished up our supper. A small snippet of liver went on her own plate, and one a bit bigger was left in the pan for Father.

First we broke up our bread, carefully picking up any crumbs made in the process to dip in the gravy. Well-behaved above the table, we gently and joyfully kicked each other underneath it. When the bread and gravy were gone, we ate our liver, licking the gravy smears where the liver had been.

'Don't put your plates in the bowl yet,' said Mam. Then from a frail she took a piece of fancy cake, the like of which we'd never seen on our table before. Plain slab was a delicate luxury, and this was no plain slab! It had two yellow layers with a pink layer in the middle, and was sandwiched together with cream and jam. Mam put a slice each on our plates and it looked too good to eat. It seemed to me like an act of wicked greed to eat cake, jam and cream in one. I longed for a piece of bread to spread the jam and cream on, but I was a coward, and waited till Mam turned her head. Silently I signalled my idea to Bess. She was bigger and braver than me and was sitting on the other side of the table, out of reach of a clip round the head for such cheek.

'Wot you two up to?' asked Mam.

''Er do want another piece o' bread.'

I cringed away, but without a grumble Mam cut us all a piece.

With delicate care we all scraped our jam and cream on to our bread, picking up the tiniest morsel of cake dropped on the table with a tongue-moistened forefinger. We made our feast last a long time.

'Jesus Christ, I be vull as a egg!' said our little brother, rubbing his stomach through the big hole in the front of his jersey. It was the first time a grace had been said at our table.

'Get the flannel from the back-kitchen and rub round their mouths ready for bed,' Mam ordered.

When that was done, she fumbled in a frail and pulled out a doll's cup and saucer made of brightly-painted tin for our little sister, and a bag of coloured clay marbles for our brother. They accepted these gifts with the same puzzled delight that Cinderella must have felt when the pumpkin turned into a fairy coach. Then Bess and I gave them a pick-a-back up the stairs, and put our little brother in the middle of the iron bedstead he shared with us, and our little sister in the home-made bed next to our parents' bed in the other room. When we got downstairs again we found there was a packet of coloured crayons for Bess, who loved to draw, and a little round box of minute multicoloured china beads for me, and, glory of glories, two comics as well – *The Rainbow* and *The Sunbeam*.

'If you two be quiet, you can stop up for a bit,' said Mam, settling herself down in the chair by the hearth for a nap.

But where had the money come from to pay for all this? I'd heard her say in desperation more than once that she wouldn't be above robbing the bank if she knew how to do it. When I was sure she was fast asleep, I whispered my fear to Bess.

'Doosn't thee fret theeself, you silly 'aporth. Our Mam could afford it. You know the bottom o'thic table leg our Dad 'ave bin a-carvin' for Mr Jones? Well, thic Mr Jones was that pleased, 'im give our Dad seven-and-sixpence for doin' it. Course, our Mam 'ad the money, but you can bet 'er got our Dad a' extra 'alf ounce o' baccy out on't.'

Well, what a lot of money to pay for a table leg to be mended! True, Dad had been ages doing it, whittling away with a pen-knife, a gouge and a chisel, to turn a block of wood into what looked like a lion's claw wreathed with flowers. A few days previously, Mam had sent me down to the shed at the bottom of our garden to tell Dad to 'look slippy, the coal 'ad bin delivered'.

'Wot d'you think o' that then, my wench?' Dad had asked me, holding up the almost finished carving.

'That's bloody good, Dad, thic rose and them leaves do look just like the shape o' real 'uns.'

'Yus, I reckon your old feyther's done a bloody masterpiece there. I bet thic Michael Anjeeloo oudn'ta' done it much better wi' the sart o' tools I've got. I reckon Mr Jones' eyes'll pop out o' 'is yud when 'im do see wot a good job I a-made on't.'

'Yus, Dad, and if thee doosn't come and start getting thic coal in, our Mam'll be making *thy* eyes pop out o' thy yud!'

We weren't wallowing in ill-gotten gains then! With my belly full of liver and fancy cake, and my fingers decked with rings of threaded beads, and *all of it paid for*, I heaved a great sigh of relief. Bess and I sat quiet as angels in the golden light from the paraffin lamp, transported into the world of Tiger Tim, Suzie Sunshine, Marzipan the Magician, and the delicious adventures of The Two Pickles.

We watched Mam till she showed signs of stirring, then tiptoed upstairs before she could order us into the cold dark back-kitchen to spoil a perfect evening with our idea of a wash.

Snuggling down under Mam's heavy home-made patchwork quilt, we drifted into contented dreams.

Despite the fact that, unlike Dad, Mam never got her head stuck in a book, she sometimes came up with an original idea that would not have entered his head. Sometimes she thought it best not to share with him, as for example, when she had the idea to go scrumping some apples.

On this occasion, I was the lucky one to whom she confided her hopes.

'Bain't stealin', really,' she said, 'you see, they've finished wi' pickin' the apples now for cider an' suchlike, an' them what's left on the ground only goes bad. You an' I could go arter dinner. 'Tis Sunday, so there won't be a lot o' people about. We can take the colander to get a few blackberries from the 'edges of the orchard, in case we do see anybody. We'll pick some elderberries for your feyther's 'erb tea as well, so everybody'll be satisfied. Mind you, it's a smart step; two miles if it's a yard, an' it's uphill all the road. What d'you say then; d'you want to come with Mam?'

My greedy little stomach would not have owned me had I turned down such an offer. Apples to munch, apples to munch, it made my mouth water to think of them.

'Not 'alf,' I agreed.

With the colander held conspicuously, and two frails rolled unobtrusively under our arms, we started out after dinner, leaving others to wash up and mind the little ones.

We went through the woodland path, the way of us children, as far as the school. Without the busy hum of children's voices, and the comings and goings of little swarms of them in and out of entrances, it had the air of an abandoned beehive.

The hill was now less steep, and was dotted with cottages. 'Nice day', 'warm for the time o' year', and a few incurious stares, and we came to the road where we forked left. Here I was on unfamiliar territory.

''Ere 'tis,' said Mam at long last, as we came to a wide, five-barred gate with a path leading down through an orchard. Sure enough, speckled among the grass under the trees, were apples; pale green ones and rosy ones, some half-bad, and some nearly all good. There were also apples here and there on the branches.

Beside the gate was a notice – *Trespassers will be Prosecuted*. Even with her glasses on, Mam was very short-sighted, and I was too distracted by the apples to give it a second thought. There was one snag; we were in view of a man working on the land on the opposite side of the road.

Mam outlined our strategy. 'We'll just go in as if we've a right to. Don't pick any apples up yet. There's sure to be some blackberries round the meadows further on. We'll go an' pick some; then when we come back out, we'll fill the frails wi' apples. Wi' a bit o' luck thic man will've gone in for 'is tea by then.'

Sure enough, the gate at the other end of this long orchard opened on to a big field that sloped up on the right to a bank with a dip behind it. A few yards down, on the left, some huge blackberry bushes tumbled over the barbed wire fence that separated the meadow from a wild copse of brambles, nettles, and tangled undergrowth.

I had popped about two blackberries in my mouth, and one in the colander, when simultaneously Mam and I became aware of the bull, which had apparently been grazing on the other side of the bank, and was now coming to charge angrily at the intruders.

'Oh, my Gawd, quick! Get over thic wire.' I had never heard Mam sound so alarmed. Without ceremony, or regard for the barbed wire, Mam heaved and pushed me over, then scrambled over herself. By then the bull was practically breathing down her neck.

Shoving, pushing, and pulling me in front of her, she gasped out to keep going; stumbling over a jungle of briars, nettles and other hindrances that clawed at us and stung. It was some yards before I looked up at Mam's face. It was pale ashen grey, lips and all, and beads of sweat had run down, misted up her glasses, and mixed with the blood from the scratches on her face.

'Was we in bad danger, Mam?' I asked.

''Im 'ould 'a killed us, but I reckon thic barbed wire fence 'ave 'alted'n. But be a good little wench and never mind the stings and scratches. The sooner we be out of 'ere the better.' Mam was so breathless it was an effort for her to speak at all.

Unable to see where we were going, we beat down a path with our arms and legs. At last we came to the end of the copse, and to a fence we could climb over on to the edge of a ploughed field. We skirted round this until we came to a gate. Over the gate, and we were on the grass verge of the road again.

'Oh, dear!' said Mam. 'What a sight you be! You do look as though you bin pulled through a 'edge back'ards.' She should have seen herself! We had lost the colander, but miraculously Mam had hung on to the frails. Very dispirited, we started home.

We were soon back by the orchard gate again. The man who had been working opposite was gone.

The apples still lay in the grass. Growing out of the hedge near the gate was an elderflower tree.

'Come on,' said Mam, pulling a few small branches of the berried elderflower to top the apples with, 'we'll dap in quick while we've got the chance, and fill the frails. Try and pick up the best ones.'

The damp grass had rotted the underside of most of them, but, noses to ground, we darted about under those trees like a pair of well-trained retrievers.

Urged by Mam to be quick, I did not even stop to eat one; anyway I intended, on the way home, to carry some of my load inside my skin. With the frails full to gaping open, we covered the apples with elderberry foliage, and were only yards from safety, when a man coming down the road turned into the gate. Our hearts sank.

With his boots and leggings, battered-brimmed hat above his weather-beaten face, he was obviously a farmer, maybe *the* farmer. Arms akimbo, legs apart, he stood blocking our way, and gruffly asked us what might we be doing in his orchard? His eyes were hard and angry.

So bedraggled were we by this time, he might well have mistaken us for a pair of gypsies.

The shape of the apples bulged out the sides of the straw frails. Red in the face as the rosiest of them, Mam tried to bluff her way out. 'We've just bin gatherin' a few 'erbs for the children's coughs in the winter; we didn't think we was doin' any 'arm.'

'Then you won't mind tipping your bags up for me to see.'

I felt deeply embarrassed, and sorry for Mam; we had escaped a bull, and as far as I could judge, had bumped into a pig. 'It's only a few 'erbs,' Mam lied lamely.

With that he picked up the frails, and tipped the apples out. Then he asked Mam for her name and address; she was near to tears when she told him.

'Pick up your bags, and don't let me catch you on my land again,' he warned us. Mam took her frails, and did not even bother to pick up the elderberries. Downcast and dejected, we carefully closed the orchard gate behind us, under the malevolent eye of the owner.

'The greedy, mingy old bugger!' I exploded, feeling that such a remark was safely above censure in the circumstances, 'all that traipsin' about an' 'ard work for nothin'!'

'Never mind,' said Mam, 'it could 'ave bin wuss. Thic bull might 'ave 'ad us. I only 'ope thic farmer's bark is wuss than 'is bite. I dread to think what'll happen if 'im do summons me. After all, 'twouldn't never do for 'im to let people come an' go on 'is land when they pick and choose. If 'im let one do it, 'undreds more 'ould do the same. The pity is that we got caught.'

Under some trees nearer home, Mam stopped, 'Might as well fill up these frails wi' these nice dry bits o' fire 'ood. They do 'elp to boil the kettle real quick for your feyther's cup o' tea on 'is early shift.'

A real mam our Mam was. Perhaps, on second thoughts, that farmer came to the same conclusion, for Mam heard no more from him.

# School

Our village straggled up each side of a steep and stony track, an offshoot from the main road. Like London, we had our West End and our East End, our slums and our grandeur. The industrious, frugal, small-familied and childless couples, who'd saved hard to build their own places, lived in an extension of the village on the side of the main road. Their little palaces were mostly wooden or stone bungalows, with ingenious little architectural trimmings that sprang from competition between their owners.

One place was particularly attractive, inside and out. The couple had only one child. I once heard a bitterly envious woman saying, 'Aye, one of the ronk 'uns, 'er is. I 'eard as 'er do tie a rag on a string and shove it up just before 'er do let 'er old mon get near 'er.'

In the gardens of the élite, snow-white washing danced on the clothes lines every Monday morning. The women never had to hide from the tradesmen and didn't patronise the packmen. Though they might give away a pair of well-polished, much-patched, worn-out boots, they were arid ground for the borrowers and cadgers. They kept primly to themselves in their prim little dwellings. They didn't laugh a lot.

At the top end of the village lived the feckless and the slummocky – and some wonderful women who had so many children they didn't know what to do next in the struggle to keep them clean, fed and clothed with the means at their disposal.

The hunger and the poverty at the feckless end, and in the middle (where *we* lived) got worse for us children when our sorely tried fathers, maddened to revolt by worsening conditions and short time in the pits, came out on strike. Soon there were no pigs in the cots, nor fowls pecking around the doors. No longer able to buy their bit of bacca, the men made themselves sick trying to smoke dried coltsfoot leaves. We children were often sick from the bitter acorns we tried desperately hard to acquire a taste for. With no pigs to snout them out, we scratched the earth away from a wild feathery-leaved plant for its bulbous root, called pignuts. Alas, these grew few and far between.

Tuberculosis followed malnutrition, and some of the village children were sent to sanatoria. Lucky things, we thought; but the rest of us had some good luck too – 'they' started free dinners at school. I don't remember who 'they' were, but I do remember the dinners. Our Mam tried to get some sort of meat for Sunday dinner, but now it was meat *every day* – beautiful stews, corned beef, mince! And pudding as well – rice pudding made with milk, jam roly-poly, and (crowning delicacy) treacle pudding. This I liked above all else. We had one helping and never expected two.

One dinner-time 'they', who organised the dinners, came and had some with us. 'They' sat at a special table with the head-master. When the tables were cleared, instead of telling us to dismiss, the headmaster stood up and said something I couldn't catch.

'What did 'im say, Bess?' I asked my elder sister.

She answered, with a sarcasm quite lost on me, 'Who do want some more treacle pud?'

Up shot my hand, surprisingly the only one. Puzzled, the head-master asked what did I want? I told him: 'More puddin', please.'

There was silence while the whole school took the shock. Two hundred pairs of eyes gave me their undivided attention.

'You sawney 'aporth!' hissed my sister adding a sharp poke in the ribs.

The headmaster was equal to the occasion. 'We can't hold up the speeches of thanks at the moment, but no doubt Cook will find a bit of extra pudding for such an appreciative little stomach.' The joke went down well, but I wished I were dead; and when we were dismissed to the playground my sister turned her back on me, disowning me for my lack of manners. I hung back, trying to look invisible till I could get out and find a corner to hide in.

The headmaster was sitting by the door. As I passed he grabbed me on to his lap. 'Come on then, my little pudding girl, Cook's got a nice big helping for you.'

Dumb with mortification, I struggled off his lap. One more crumb of treacle pudding and I should have choked.

His name was Mr High, but in fact he was very short, and also very stout. His stomach protruded like a balloon blown up to bursting point. It was commonly said that if you could tap his navel, you would turn on undiluted cider. He was never actually sober nor ever completely drunk.

If he was a walking cider barrel, his wife was a tall vinegar bottle. They hated each other with cold, polite venom. They had no child-ren, which may have been the root of the matter. It was a matter of opinion whether she had driven him to drink by her sour nature, or had acquired her sourness because of his drinking.

He was much the kinder of the two. As long as the pupils scraped through the low standards of learning required by the schools inspectors, he was not much concerned with our education. I think he considered the raw material at his disposal was not worth much cultivation.

When he required the labour, older pupils were sent to gather kindling wood for his home fires, sacks of bracken for his pigs' bedding, leaf-mould for his garden, and blackberries for his wife's preserves. These activities passed for nature study.

Mostly he treated us all with good-natured sarcasm, but now and again, when he was taking a class, he went into one of his tantrums. When he felt a tantrum coming on, the slightest misdemeanour, real or unintended, would set him off. Forms and desks toppled over as he dragged us out, clouting us round the ears with one hand, wielding his stick with the other. He threw our exercise books in the air, and pages came flying all over the classroom. It always gave me a fit of the giggles; I knew he would be likely to bring a chair down on my head if he noticed, so I always bent down to tie up my bootlaces during the hurricane. That way I got my whacks along my back. He never favoured anyone; we all got a hiding when he was in the mood. It did him the world of good – he was well-behaved for a long time afterwards.

Mrs High, who taught Standard Three, was a born snob; she only had time for the very small percentage of clean, tidy children. A runny-nosed, dirty, raggedy child like me appeared to contaminate her. She particularly disliked any child the headmaster especially noticed. (Poor woman! God knows what jealousies racked her soul.) On both counts I was doomed. When I reached Standard Three, at the age of nine, I was already Mr High's little pudding girl, and I was at all times an offence to the eye in the extraordinary assortment of clothes our Mam gave me to wear. But, by a piece of luck such as seldom came my way, I was out of the class again before the year was out.

As Mrs High took no interest in the scruffier members of her class, I was able to spend my time drawing, doodling and composing rhymes in my exercise book; and one afternoon, when Mr High made one of his rare visits to Standard Three to look over our work, he picked up my book and said, 'How's my little pudding girl getting on?'

'I'll cop it now,' I thought, and wasn't surprised when he told me to come to the front of the class. However should I hold up my head again if he gave me the cane? It was a punishment rarely administered, which made the boys heroes, if they didn't yell or grimace, but disgraced a girl for the rest of her school life.

Instead of caning me, Mr High told me to read out some of my work to the class; and then he marched me into the top class, where Standards Five and Six were taught by Miss Hale. Bess was in this class. I waited while he had a little chat with Miss Hale; then I was told to step up on to her blackboard platform and read my poems out again. It appeared I'd done something clever. The pupils laughed a lot when I finished.

It took very little encouragement to inflate my ego, but later Bess said, 'It was your drawers. That leg with the 'lastic out was all 'angin' down.' And Mrs High's expression when I returned to her class damped down any further poetic aspirations and stopped me getting conceited.

Nevertheless, the following Monday I skipped Standard Four and was put into Miss Hale's class. It was soon obvious that I was an absolute duffer at arithmetic and sewing, but the humiliation of being bottom of the class in these subjects was made up for by Miss Hale's reading to us. She took us out of the classroom, over the hills and far away, with *Uncle Tom's Cabin, Black Beauty, Lorna Doone, Treasure Island*. This wasn't just 'doing the classics' – as she went along, we followed spellbound. Every day, life became richer. Learning new words was like having a key to free the imprisoned thoughts I'd been unable to express. And Miss Hale was always ready to listen.

Besides, she never commented on the weird unsuitability of our clothes, she never appeared even to notice the dried soapflakes on our necks, camouflaging the fleabites. Going to school now became a wonderful daily treat.

Another treat that came my way about the same time was when I was given a pile of schoolgirl magazines called *The Bluebird*. They came from Goggy, a boy who hadn't been able to go to work in the pits like the other boys, because he had so much wrong with him. His whole body was covered with taut, angry red skin as though he'd been scalded. His watery, raw-rimmed eyes were nearly blind. He had to wear special shoes for his misshapen sore feet, and even in these walking was an uncomfortable process. Inside this grotesque exterior was a wonderful young man, kind, intelligent, and purposeful.

He earned his living doing a paper round. Daily it took him over a large area of scattered cottages, single and in clusters, and it took him all God's hours to walk the umpteen miles on his tender feet.

His wage was ten shillings a week. His widowed mother Mrs Protheroe acted midwife and washerwoman, or layer-out of the dead, to any villager that could spare a shilling or two for such services. She did it for nothing for those she respected if they had nothing to pay with. She made an art of frugality, wasting nothing, and kept herself and Goggy adequately fed and housed and very, very clean.

She and Goggy are both dead now, but they'll always be on the short list of those I have truly loved.

Anyway, Goggy gave me this treasure – this pile of schoolgirl magazines, which I had difficulty in hiding from the ravaging hands of the little ones, from the teasing destruction of older children, and most of all from Mam. Mam never read anything. Paper, to her, was something to be stuffed into holey boots, to spread on the table instead of a cloth, to protect the freshly scrubbed flagstone floor from our muddy tread, to lay fires with, or cut into squares for hanging in the privy. (The frustrations I suffered from reading unfinished snippets in there!)

The privy was my seat of learning. There I could stay for long sessions of undisturbed reading, and escape into fantasy. While my craze for those *Bluebird* magazines lasted, I became in turn Lil of the Lighthouse, Wanda of the Movies, the Heroine of St Catherine's, and even the Richest Girl in the School. Now and again, for a change, I was just myself.

# Chapel

Mondays and Fridays we mixed with other children of the village at school, and on Sundays we met most of them again at chapel.

The chapel stood on a small natural plateau roughly in the middle of the village. We were told it was God's house, but we didn't think *He* would have much time to visit our chapel in person.

The chapel was looked after by a couple of the most respected villagers, and was kept clean and polished by Mrs Protheroe.

We knew we had to mind our P's and Q's in there, but it was a small and friendly house, with no pretensions of grandeur. It did not feel hollow and cold, nor at all overpowering. The windows were of plain glass, and bursts of sunshine brought out extra gleams on the wooden forms polished with such fervour by Mrs Protheroe.

It was quite pleasant to go there on wet Sundays and cold Wednesday evenings. We could still enjoy ourselves, and pass muster with the Sunday school teachers, even with our attention divided between them and our mischief.

The chapel did not have a ghoulish graveyard, either. Our Methodist preachers tried to take care of our souls, but the church, a couple of miles away, had to dispose of our mortal remains.

A simple place, our chapel, yet when the congregation joined together in a full-throated rendering of a favourite hymn, many of us shared a true communion with each other.

The women from the better-off end of the village and a sprinkling of the husbands were regular chapel-goers. Not so the other end. All too often the poorer women 'hadn't a rag on their backs good enough for chapel!'

We were the in-betweens in chapel attendance too, but every so often the love of music in Mam's Welsh blood drew her to chapel on a Sunday evening for the joy of the hymn singing.

'You can come with Mam, if you like,' she would offer me

kindly. This would put me in a bit of a quandary. It didn't seem nice to refuse what Mam thought was a treat, and I knew it was likely that she would have a sweet or two in the bottom of her pocket to cure the fidgets brought on by the sermon.

Of course, in the hymn singing, there was the fascinating study of rows of faces, full of mouth-holes of infinite variety, pulled into the most peculiar shapes to get the tunes out. There was trying to count up to a hundred between the sonorous 'amens' of old Mr Matton; and there was the ribbon boss on the front of Mrs Griffiths' hat, which always looked as though it was going to fall off, but didn't. There were, too, mimes to make to other young sufferers in other rows, who had been conned into attending.

Some evenings I did go with Mam, but on other occasions the afternoon at Sunday school seemed more than enough for one day. Very few of us attended Sunday school for its own sake, but if we didn't put in a minimum number of appearances in the year, we wouldn't be included in the chapel treat.

But Sunday school – and attendances there – bucked up a bit when we had the novelty of a new teacher. This lady, Mrs Smith, was middle-aged with the gentlest voice and manner. I thought she had a beautiful face. She wore her hair in a bun, and when the sunlight came through the chapel window it lit up the tendrils of hair round her forehead into a golden halo. Instead of just reading from the Bible, she told us charming little stories. The boys tried to spoil it by asking her to read those parts of the Bible containing the 'dirty bits' they'd found out about. I felt very sorry for her, pink-faced and embarrassed, trying to ignore them. It was small martyrdom compared with what came later.

It was not an unknown sin, and men here and there committed it, but a woman? Never! Well, not until it came to light that Mrs Smith did. Yes, she was a female gambler! She put money on horses!

Secrets had a short life in our village. The preacher soon heard of this backslider brought into our midst. Justice must be done, and heard to be done, from the pulpit, in the Lord's name.

Unaware of all this, Mrs Smith took her seat among the Sunday-evening congregation. The chapel was much fuller than usual – sadists that we were.

Starting off in his low-pitched, holier-than-thou quaver, the preacher soon worked himself into a volcanic eruption of denouncement against those who committed one of the basest sins against their Maker – the sin of gambling. And who could be a greater sinner than a sister who had succumbed to this lure of the Devil?

So the ashes fell on her unprepared, defenceless head! There was a long dramatic pause, as long as he could manage to hold it without losing our attention. Then, again in low-pitched quavers, he asked the congregation to kneel and pray that the sinner in our midst might be brought back to righteousness by repentance and washed clean again in the blood of the Lamb. She must have been a compulsive gambler for she stopped coming to chapel. Dad never went to chapel, but he said he'd gamble a sovereign to a penny that Mrs Smith had more chance of getting to heaven than that preacher.

Chapel treat used to come on a school day, and as far as we were concerned the teacher might as well not have been there that day – our attention was on the classroom clock. Would it never come round to two o'clock? The rumble of empty stomachs was louder than the scratching of desultory pens, or the buzzing of lethargic bees and flies round the jam jars of wild flowers on the window-sills. Most of the mothers, knowing their offspring would get full bellies at the treat tea, gave them no food for the midday play break.

At last, when the hands of the clock said two precisely, the teacher would tell us to line up in front of the class and dismiss in a quiet and orderly fashion. Anyone disobeying would be brought back to class and miss the treat. We shuffled out as quietly as our nailed boots would allow, with never a whisper between us until we were clear of the school yard. Then, mad as a bunch of March hares, yelling and hooting at the top of our voices, we rushed as fast as our legs would carry us, through the wood to home.

Most of us were indoors only long enough to get our hair combed, face and hands washed, and stockings pulled up. We had nothing to change into. A few lucky ones had the paper curlers taken out of their hair, ribbon bows tied on, and fresh clean dresses. Then off to the chapel where we sat in rows on a grassy slope and the Minister came out to hear us say grace: 'For what we are about to receive may the Lord make us truly thankful.'

The words didn't do justice to our feelings. For many of us it was the only meal of the year that offered the luxury of eating as much as we wanted. And what a feast it was! For a start, what bread! Not bread like we had at home – kept for a few days before cutting, to make it go further, then spread only in the middle with lard, marge or lumpy mutton dripping, and strictly rationed to one or two pieces. *This* bread was oven-fresh, only a quarter-inch thick, cut from long squares and spread all over – corner to corner

– with golden best butter. The Diamond Jubilee mugs were filled with scalding hot tea; and no one stinged with the milk and sugar. Like goddesses with cornucopias three village matrons bustled in and out of the vestry with an everlasting supply of baskets and enamel jugs. 'Don't know where the young varmints be putting it all,' they would laugh to one another, their kindly faces beaming under Sunday hats. As it was a chapel do, it had to be respected by Sunday hats, although they wore starched white aprons over their dark dresses.

Not until we all had agreed among ourselves that we 'wuz as vull as eggs' did we concede we were ready for a slice of bright slab cake. After such bounty we yelled our Thank-you grace.

Next we lined up behind the 'band' – that is, anyone who could play a mouth organ, tin whistle, a jew's harp, or even a paper and comb. We did a lap of honour round the village so that those too old or infirm to join us shouldn't miss the sight, and then down to the main road (where a motor car was still something to stand and stare at), to march singing at the top of our voices, in and out of tune, to the only farm in the district. Here the farmer let us have the use of one of his fields for our fun and games.

I was never any good at the egg-and-spoon, three-legged or sack races: after a flash start my stamina gave out completely. But I did win the penny prize in the bun-eating contest. For this a rope was fixed between two stakes and buns hung from it on a string. With hands tied behind our backs, we had to kneel down to catch and eat a bun. ''Tain't fair – 'er do allus win cos 'er got a chops twice as big as anybody else's,' said the rosebud mouths I envied all the rest of the year. For once I was glad I'd got a genuine 'cake hole'. I spent my prize money straight away on an ice-cream cornet, giving the first licks to my little brother and sister.

When our games were finished, the grown-ups followed suit, frolicking like children, falling over in the sack and three-legged race, laughing and making fools of themselves to our huge delight.

Just when the running about and excitement had made us thirsty and peckish again, the three matrons would be spied coming up the road with the remains of the bread and butter in baskets and a couple of helpers with big cans of cold tea. Then, before their legs were too tired to carry them, the very young and the very old took each other home, carrying with them bunches of cowslips picked from the meadow, thus leaving the field clear for the evening game of 'kiss in the ring'. This offered the one chance of flirtation that village convention allowed. Everyone made the most of it, and maybe when dusk fell the kissing lingered longer, and maybe the hugging got a bit tighter. But that was as far as it went; husbands and wives, sweethearts and lovers, went home in their proper pairs. A few men felt more manly, a few women more feminine, but some were more lonely than ever.

Another yearly treat run by the chapel was the Teetotallers' outing. Our virtuous reputation as teetotallers was quite un-earned; we never had the chance or money to be anything else; except when some boys at school found that the headmaster hadn't locked the shed where he kept his barrels of cider. There, after school, he found five boys in a state of maudlin drunkenness when he was fetching his own supply. The boys were banned from the Good Templars meetings and from the outing; but being boys, it wasn't much disgrace. They would grow into men. Alcohol was only a sin for women and children. If a drop of cider did come a woman's way, she warmed it on the hob and drank it as 'medicine'.

The Teetotallers' outing was a grand affair. We could hardly contain our pride as we waited at the bottom of the village for the char-à-banc. What travellers we were! It was a good twenty-mile ride to our destination, a privately owned playground at Bishops Cleeve. We had the excitement of going through Gloucester, and also the privilege (as I considered – for the likes of us) of being allowed to pass through Cheltenham, with its grand Georgian houses and wide tree-lined roads.

Once, as we were going up Lansdown Road, Mrs Toomey saw her daughter, Emma, coming out of one of the houses, with some letters: obviously sent to the post by her employer. Of course it was unthinkable for the char-à-banc driver to stop so that Emma's Mam and her brothers and sisters could give her a hug and a kiss! But they caught sight of each other and waved frantically; and the other women made quite a do of how smart young Emma looked in her cap and apron, while Mrs Toomey fumbled around for something to dab her eyes with.

The playground we went to wasn't a brightly painted affair; everything had a weather-beaten drabness. But there were see-saws, roundabouts, helter-skelters, and swings. With our threepence entrance fee, we had freedom to go on everything. A tea was laid on in a big wooden hut; not unlimited like the chapel treat tea, but all the same a satisfying number of pieces of bread and butter, a small fancy cake apiece, and two cups of tea. It was stylish too, for we sat on long wooden benches, and ate off trestle tables.

We squeezed the last minute from this outing; we left only when the early September dusk stopped play. It was very thrilling for those of us who could keep awake to see Cheltenham and Gloucester with their lights on. The older children nursed the sleeping younger ones and sang all the way home:

Pull for the shore, sailor, pull for the shore
Heed not the rolling waves, but bend to the oar
– our favourite hymn.

Teetotallers we may have been, but the after-effects of the swings, see-saws, and roundabouts, sent us reeling up our garden paths like a lot of drunken sailors.

One year, when I was about nine, I caught a strong dose of religious mania. It didn't last very long, and it was after I'd read a book called *Teddy's Button*. I kept my conversion a secret with God, because I didn't want to be laughed at, but the incredible improvement in my behaviour caused Mam to get quite worried. Well-behaved children were often marked for an early grave.

Actually it was a very handy time for me to believe in God and his miracles; I badly needed a miracle to fit me up with suitable clothes for Chapel Anniversary Sunday. Nearly everybody in the village made an effort to attend the anniversary, to see their daughters sing and recite in a service to mark the occasion.

Never backward to seize a chance to hog the limelight, I learned a fourteen-verse poem of religious platitudes, with which to try the Christian patience of the congregation. Its sheer length gave me the leading role, but I was desperately short of costume for the part.

Ideally, each girl should have been dressed all in white: a rare achievement indeed in our community. With my new-found faith in God's omnipotence, I thought this time I might be lucky. He could raise people from the dead, He could feed thousands on a handful of fish and three loaves; in that case He could provide me with some anniversary clothes. Nothing is beyond the power of prayer, and I prayed: morning, noon and night, promising God I would keep up my good behaviour, and would He please oblige me with an angel bringing a white silk frock, white straw hat (with ribbons), and white shoes and socks. White canvas shoes would do, I didn't expect buckskin. So that nobody would know of the arrangement, the angel could leave them in the fox-hole by the chestnut tree, and I would go out to play and 'find' them after school.

With pounding heart, I approached the hole every day; it was empty. Serve me right I thought! I'd been too greedy, asked too much. I amended my request. It could be a blue frock, a very plain hat, and brown shoes would do; and it wouldn't matter if none of it was new.

By Saturday, eve of the great day, I was still praying, but I would have settled for anything, provided I looked tidy. Nothing appeared, even though I raked thoroughly among the dead oak leaves, in case the angel had hidden my things from prying eyes.

I wished now that I hadn't given my brother the whole piece of orange peel that a girl had given me at school. I would have kept some for myself, had I known God was so mingy with His miracles. I looked up at the sky, and for Anyone who was looking I gave one of my awful scowls.

Reduced now to a weeping nuisance of self-pity, I went indoors and drove Mam beside herself by fretting about what I should wear on the next day.

Mam was so desperate that as a last hope she suggested we should try the Reddings. The Redding family were distant relations who had a small draper's shop, and in our eyes they were people of consequence. We had no friendship or contact with this grand family, who certainly wished none with us.

I was to go and ask them politely if they had any clothes to spare, as Mam couldn't get me any this week, what with Dad's pit boots falling to pieces, and her having to buy cough medicine for my little brother. 'Mind you,' she warned me, 'you might be unlucky, for people do say they be too mean to gi' you the time o' day.'

It was a long walk – over two miles – and I had time to ponder. Perhaps God had put the idea into Mam's head, for didn't He work in mysterious ways His wonders to perform? So I prayed again; all the way through the woods, along the main road, and through the straggling hamlet of Drybrook, till I came to the Reddings' garden gate. I was very thirsty and very hungry, but I tried to assume a polite and pleasant expression before asking for their bounty.

Old Mrs Redding answered my knock. She was small and bony, and she wore a voluminous black skirt, black blouse and a crochet shawl of red, blue and yellow. I thought she looked like a bantam hen.

All Mam had told me to say came out in a rush of supplication. The old lady didn't look very pleased. She didn't say anything, but hemmed and hawed in a very discouraging manner, and then went back indoors. She didn't ask me to step inside, but she didn't close the door either, so I waited hopefully on the doorstep.

After some time, she returned, carrying a bulky brown paper

parcel tied so that the string would form a carrying handle. I could see the shape of a hat in it. I truly thanked her from the bottom of my heart, and decided not to take any further advantage by asking for a drink of water. I couldn't hurry through that hamlet quick enough to get to a quiet piece of road and undo the string, and see what I had got. I kept beaming skywards, my imagination full of white silk, lace and ribbons. But I was practically an unbeliever after I'd opened that parcel.

It contained two hats, one inside the other, and a frock. The style of the frock was all right, for I liked a bit of novelty; it was too big, though that didn't much matter either, but the colours! Black and brown! The top was made up of alternate squares of black and brown silk, like a chessboard, faggot-stitched together. The skirt was formed of three frills, two black, and a brown one in the middle. It was hard work, looking for a silver lining in that dress, but it *was* silk, and I was sure the skirt would make a big flounce if I twirled round in it. There were no shoes, but I supposed that my black boots would match the dress. Anyway, beggars couldn't be choosers.

The hats were a better proposition. They were identical in shape, made out of bands of straw braid. Both had faded to a dusty dark grey, but where the ribbons had been removed, I could see one had been a bright pink, the other cream.

I was suddenly inspired – I would undo the braid and turn it to the clean side on the pink hat. No, better still, I would unpick the braid from *both* hats and sew it in alternate stripes, clean side uppermost. I forgot how hungry and tired I was, as I hurried home to get on with my project.

Mam was pleased I'd struck lucky. She'd been fortunate too, while I was out. Gladys's mum had given her a basin of home-cured lard, and she spread some on two thick slices of bread for me. It was delicious with a sprinkle of salt. She let me finish up the tea in the pot, and then brought out a pair of brown sandals. They were not new, and the backs had been trodden down, never to stand again. They were also a bit too big; but providing I shuffled along without lifting my feet, I could manage. I was thrilled to bits. Hitherto my footwear had always been boots – often nailed boots; sandals were dainty and glamorous.

My spirits were high enough before Mam showed me the nearly-white socks that Mrs Brown had given her to go with the sandals. 'Thy cup runneth over,' I thought to myself.

The snag was Mrs Brown's stuck-up daughter, Eunice; she might throw it up at me about Mam asking for her old shoes. 'You never *cadged* 'em, did you, Mam?'

'No, that I didn't. I just 'appened to mention that you 'adn't a shoe fit to wear tomorrer, and she fetched them sandals and socks and gave 'em to me.'

Comforted on that point, I rummaged around looking for sewing cotton. The reel was nearly empty, but Mam let me pull threads from a treasured wash-stand cloth she used when the babies came. But the threads weren't very strong. I cut the pink and cream braid on the hats into pieces, sewed them together and wound them round into a hat shape, putting in a fixing stitch as often as the thread would allow.

Frayed edges were much in evidence, and my little brother said the hat looked like a 'busted bee skep'. In my eyes, it was a creation of no mean beauty. Mam let me stand it, for safety, on the wash-stand jug in her bedroom.

Because I could only shuffle along in my sandals, I started for chapel well before time. We had to wait in the little vestry; then make a grand entrance into chapel. When I arrived, a few girls were there already, among them Eunice.

I detested Eunice. I couldn't understand why God singled her out for so many favours. She was a cribber at school, put the blame for her own misdeeds on other children, and gave weak-minded cronies bites of bread and jam out of her lunch box. When she had a fight, she was downright spiteful.

There she sat today, clad from top to toe in white, except for the pink rosebuds and blue forget-me-nots round her straw hat. She had long brown curls as well, and a pretty face. There couldn't have been much left for her to ask God for. It didn't seem fair!

Gladys, my best friend, was there, and she too was nearly all in white, but I didn't mind about her. Gladys could have been dressed in fairy gossamer, and I wouldn't have grudged her it. She was kind and nice to everybody, especially me. She patted the place on the wooden form next to her for me to sit down.

All the glory I had felt in my sandals, white socks, and straw hat (which I'd thought quite passable with the frayed ends at the back) vanished. Compared with the others, I was going to look a proper gypsy. I just managed to hold back the tears and make a concentrated study of my whitish socks.

Presently Nell Wills shuffled in. It wasn't her shoes that handicapped *her*. It was her dress!

Nell had eleven brothers and sisters. A couple of the girls were in service, and a couple of the boys worked down the pit when there was any work. All the same, it was a miracle where Nell's mum had found the money to buy the white material and lace edging for Nell's dress. Considering Mrs Wills was mother of twelve children, she hadn't much notion of relating the shape of the dress to the body's needs. It was just a straight tube with two smaller straight tubes sewn in for sleeves, and a hole left in the top for Nell's head to go through.

The lace edging had gone round the neck and sleeves, but only two-thirds round the narrow skirt bottom. This had been made even narrower by a one-sided tuck, so that the lace might fit. The whole gave an interesting lop-sided effect, and it also made it nearly impossible for Nell to walk. Still, it did have the glory of being all white. I would gladly have swopped my dark flounces for it.

'I like your frock,' purred Queen Cat Eunice to Nell.

Nell was equal to the taunt. 'Yes, my mam paid four-and-elevenpence for it, brand-new at the Bon Marché.' Nell was the sort of red-haired, brother-toughened girl you didn't call a liar!

Any pleasure I'd anticipated from reciting my poem had evaporated before I took my seat, conscious that my outlandish appearance spoilt the show.

Several girls said their pieces. Eunice, who could play the piano and had a surprisingly sweet voice for such a nasty person, sang a solo to her own accompaniment. The audience was obviously highly impressed, but now we fell from the sublime to the ridiculous, for it was my turn!

I started off well enough, and everyone suffered me with quiet politeness. Too quiet; I could hear a faint crackling noise coming from my hat. It was difficult to concentrate on my pious poem, wondering what was happening up there on my head; and it became even more difficult when I saw the big ribbon boss on Mrs Dee's hat begin to shake. She was shaking too, with suppressed laughter. She was enormously fat, and her face went the same colour as her strawberry pink frock. One of my aunties had once brought home from service a funny-shaped dish, and had made in it something called blancmange. As I watched Mrs Dee, she reminded me of the saucerful of that lovely pudding my auntie had given me, and I forgot my lines.

Like the rippling of a breeze in a cornfield, her laughter spread to everyone in the audience. I knew now what they were laughing at – my hat. The inadequate stitching must have come undone, and I could picture the braid standing up in a spiral above it.

The poor choirmaster, who'd spent patient weeks coaching us for this day, was sticking his chin in and out in nervous bewilderment at this collapse of events. I felt terribly guilty, but the whole thing seemed so comical. So I had a fit of giggles and laughed till the tears came, then sat down. The closing hymn was 'Jesus Loves Me'. Even if I hadn't been so choked up, I wouldn't have had the nerve to sing it.

I was in no hurry to go home, for I'd caught sight of Mam's red, embarrassed face in the congregation. On this special Sunday there was jelly for tea, but not even for this quivering delicacy would I go home; at least not till Dad had put in a good word for me, as I knew he would once he'd heard all about it.

I didn't have much trouble avoiding people after chapel. No one seemed to be aware of me. I hung back in the vestry till everyone had gone. Now I wanted to indulge in my panacea for all my troubles, a day-dream in the Forest. I knew a special little bank among the ferns and foxgloves formed almost like a seat. In this green enchantment, I could grow rich, beautiful and successful, paying my debts with unstinted magnanimity. Besides, I also wanted to have a good cry.

I had reckoned without Gladys. She was waiting outside with Florence Cassons, who was almost as nice as Gladys. The sympathy on their faces was too much, and I started blubbering there and then. They put their arms around me. 'Doosn't thee cry,' comforted Gladys, 'I reckon they all enjoyed themselves.'

Florence was a rather special sort of girl. For a start she lived nearly a mile from the village, at Nelsons Green, where their only neighbour was an old witch, but Florence wasn't a bit afraid of her.

To take my mind off my troubles, Gladys suggested that we should walk part of the way home with Florence, but first she'd run indoors and tell her mam. She returned with some pieces of string and tied my sandals on firmly with deft fingers. I could now lift my feet without leaving my shoes behind. My spirits lifted too. I put my 'model' hat on the end of my sandal, and kicked it back to the Devil. Florence caught my mood. 'Let's 'ave a goo on the swing tree!'

The swing tree stood beside a large shallow hole in the woods; one of the branches of a huge oak had half broken off, and was hanging by its bark and woody sinews. The end hung low enough for us to reach, hold on to, and after a quick run, let our feet off the ground and swing over the hole in a circle back to the tree. Gladys didn't want to be a spoilsport but she was a bit worried about her best white dress.

Florence had a new blue frock, but ran on to the tree for first go, without giving it a thought. She was half-way over the hole when she lost her grip. Her fall was broken by the thick carpet of dead leaves in the bottom of the hole, and by her dress which was caught in the rough end of the branch. But she'd ricked her ankle, and it hurt badly to put her foot to the ground.

I felt I was a jinx, bringing trouble and calamity to everyone. What could I do to make amends? 'Will your mam gi' you a good 'iding for ripping your frock?' Gladys asked anxiously. Florence nodded – up and down, and sideways, since she couldn't be sure.

'*You* needn't come,' I said to Gladys, 'but *I'm* goin' to take Florence all the way home.' Perhaps old Mimey the witch would have me, but I'd have to risk it, *and* her geese! My sister, Bess, had told me in strictest confidence that they weren't really geese; but people Mimey had bewitched. Perhaps she would turn me into a goose. If she did, *I* wouldn't stick my neck out and run at people to frighten them.

Even the grown-ups reckoned that Mimey was a witch; hadn't Josh Pudge lost his leg in the pit after she'd cursed him for stealing one of her fowls?

If only I could save poor Florence from a good hiding as well! I was quite a skilful little liar when I put my mind to it. I concocted a story about a ferocious dog chasing us. In our rush to escape, Florence had stumbled over a tree root.

To my great relief, Gladys bravely said she'd come all the way, or at least till the geese started for us.

Actually the geese were grazing on the far side of the green, and took no notice of our approach at all. Mrs Cassons did, and came running out from her garden to see why Florence was limping. Florence began to cry and her mam was so concerned about her swollen ankle that I only had to tell a little fib that Florence had fallen down. There was Mrs Cassons comforting Florence and telling her not to worry about her dress – she could mend it so that it would hardly show!

Now we had a bigger surprise. Old Mimey the witch came out with two pieces of blackberry-jam tart still warm from the oven – one for Gladys and one for me. I was too scared to be good-mannered enough to refuse such generosity. 'Go on, try it,' she cackled. Gladys hung back, but I took a bite, partly to humour old Mimey, partly because I was almost permanently hungry. The pastry had a melt-in-the-mouth lightness, and there was a thick filling of sweet, juicy blackberry jam.

'It's the best tart I've ever tasted,' I said truthfully. 'My mam's a wonderful old tarter, but you're an even better'un.' This compliment pleased her so much she laughed until her dewlaps shook, and you could see the dirt embedded in her criss-cross wrinkled neck.

Despite our welcome, we left Nelsons Green behind as fast as we could. Gladys hadn't touched her tart. 'I can't abide blackberries cooked,' she said, 'you 'ave it.'

'Be you quite sure?'

She nodded. I couldn't have taken it off anyone else without much more persuasion. But I knew Gladys's mam was rich enough to give her bread and jam and any time she asked for it; we wouldn't have dreamt of that in our family.

Filled with tart, I wasn't worried if there wasn't much for tea at home. I left Gladys at her gate and made my way to our cottage. Bess and her friend were playing hopscotch on the play-flattened hard earth outside our garden gate.

'Thee bisn't 'alf gonna cop it off your mam for makin' sich a gawbee o' theeself in chapel,' Bess's friend warned me.

I waited until I was inside the gate with the catch down, then pushed out my purple tongue at them.

'Pooh, I don't care, I've just 'ad *two* pieces o' jam tart to yut.'

'Fibber!'

'No I bain't. Gladys an' I took Florence Cassons wum, cos 'er sprained 'er ankle, an' old Mimey the witch gi'ed us the tart. Gladys wasn't 'ungry so 'er gi'ed I 'ers.'

'Thee'st what? Thee'st yut vittles off old Mimey! Thou silly cooten thee! Now thee'lt die at twelve o'clock tonight. 'Er only gi' thee that tart to pizen thee!'

This dramatic comment from her friend made my sister's eyes widen to their fullest concern. The bit of flattery I felt at this was soon dispelled as she calmly went on playing hopscotch. I walked soberly up the garden path. So I was going to die then. What a day it had been! Dying seemed a fitting finish to it. But anyway, midnight was a long way off.

Mam had saved me a saucerful of jelly, and a couple of yards off the end of her tongue to go with it. I let her lather herself out, without my usual impudence of sticking up for myself. Gloating in my martyrdom, I thought how sorry she would feel when she found me dead and cold in the morning.

Bess slept on the outside of the bed, my little brother in the middle, and I on the side against the wall. That wall gave me claustrophobia for life.

The other two were soon fast asleep. I listened fearfully for the chimes from Great-Aunt Lizzie's wall clock downstairs. It kept time right to the second.

I heard it strike eleven ominously. 'Matthew, Mark, Luke and John, bless the bed that I lie on. Two at my head, two at my feet, they will guard me while I sleep.'

The top of our iron bedstead was jammed against the wall, and so was my side; still I supposed angels didn't need any room as they weren't solid like us. I wondered how they would come to fetch me – through the tiny window, or through the walls? I tried to picture what it would be like to be dead. I wouldn't be able to feel anything, smell anything, hear, taste, or see anything. I was already in the pitch dark, so I knew what it was like not to see. If I couldn't do all those things, and my body had to be left behind, anyway, to go down the pity 'ole, there didn't seem much left worth taking. It was wicked to be afraid of angels; but I was. I put my head under the heavy patchwork quilt. I didn't want to see them coming into the bedroom.

The next thing I heard was Mam's irate voice threatening to come upstairs and 'larrup our arses if we wasn't down in two shakes of a lamb's tail to get ready for school.'

Her nagging voice sounded like the chimes of heaven. I wasn't dead; I was still here! I hugged my little brother fiercely.

'Pooh,' I goaded Bess, 'I bain't dead. I be still 'ere.'

Obviously the two pieces of blackberry tart still rankled, for she said: 'Ow d'you know you be? You might only think you be!' Then, jumping smartly out of bed, she hid behind the door as Mam rushed in. When Mam had finished with my bare behind, I knew I was still alive all right – and fairly tingling with it.

# Great-Aunt Lizzie

The cottage we lived in was the property of my Great-Aunt Lizzie, and she slept in our tiny parlour, having long been too crippled with arthritis to get up the stairs. Apart from her iron bed, there was a wooden chair and a chest of drawers in her room. This chest, of mahogany, with fine glass knobs, was the grandest piece of furniture in the cottage.

Old Auntie lived, with rigid independence, on her old age pension of five shillings, for which munificence she frequently and fervently thanked Lloyd George. She did accept a share of our garden produce, but more than paid for this by helping all she could with the housework, although her gnarled and misshapen hands made her slow and awkward. Often she would drat the infernal rheumatics and wish it to Halifax. We didn't know where this was, but it sounded dramatic.

Whenever she sat down, there was always a baby to go on her lap, and her voluminous fusty black skirts were our refuge when Mam was after us for some mischief. She wore black cloth boots, with shiny toe-caps that didn't protect her corns from our clumsy feet. Often, accidentally, we made her cry out with pain. She forgave us anything, and one of the treats of our lives was the weekly share of scraping out her Nestlé's milk tin. With a teaspoon each, two or three of us would take a turn on the sparse leavings till the tin was as shiny and clean inside as a new one.

Another of Auntie's bounties came after the annual visit of a middle-aged relative. He always brought her a quarter of humbugs and a few apples. This visit was not regarded by her as one of goodwill. She disliked the man over some episode in the past, and besides, she knew he had taken out an insurance policy on her life. 'I bet I be aggravatin' the varmint, lastin' this long,' she would chuckle, "im do only come to see if I be on me last legs. "'ow be you?" 'im do ex I, but what 'im's a-really sayin', by the look in 'is eyes, is "'ow dare you kip goin' on and on, an' costin' me tuppence a year for 'umbugs?" Durn me if it ain't a reg'lar tonic to me to aggravate'n so. I do feel quite perky agyun arter 'im a' bin 'ere.'

The sight of the apples and sweets perked us up too. One of the apples was cut up and shared between us as soon as he had gone. The other few Auntie stored among her laying-out clothes in the chest of drawers. It was another great treat when she cut up one of these between us, though they always tasted of camphor balls.

The Almighty, in whose existence she had implicit belief, had been more generous with her life-span than she'd anticipated. So every couple of years she paid a village woman sixpence to launder her laying-out clothes, because the coal dust from the fires got into everything. She wouldn't give our mother the task, as Mam was not the most skilful of washerwomen.

When she got into her eighties, Aunt Lizzie would gently chide the Almighty for His tardiness in collecting her. 'I be getting useless down 'ere now, and me laying-out things'll be wore out afore I, if He ben't careful.'

From her memories, and from what Dad told us, we learned a lot about her life. When she was eight years old, the eldest of four, her mother had died with the baby in childbirth. Her father worked in a stone quarry for a pittance. Straight away, with help from neighbours, little Lizzie tried to run the household. When a near-blind widow came to live in the village, and was willing to step into the role of stepmother, it seemed like an act of providence. Lizzie, now gone nine years old, thought differently. She was a better judge than her elders, and saw behind the veneer of pious goodness the cruel, greedy hypocrite her stepmother turned out to be. Too late, Lizzie's father found his mistake. So he decided it would be best for all concerned if his little wench went into service at once.

A job was found for her as scullery-maid in a manor house nearly thirty miles away. Her clothes were tied in a bundle at each end of a stick on her father's shoulder; and they set out at dawn to walk the distance. When Lizzie's legs could carry her no further, a night's shelter in a barn was begged from a farmer. The next day they tramped on, and when at length he'd handed her over to the cook, Lizzie's dad turned, with tears in his eyes, for the long walk back.

Her former life was soon almost obliterated by her new below-stairs world of dungeon cellars and labyrinthine passages, and by her lowly status among the small army of servants. In order for her to stand at the sink and reach the mountain of pots and pans she scoured, she had to get on a box. But she was not born to be a scullery-maid for long: her sturdiness of spirit, and her intelligence and shrewdness, saved her.

By the time she was sixteen, she was head housemaid, owned a locked cash-box containing golden sovereigns (her hoarded wages), and was soon to become, by a series of tragedies, a woman of property.

She had judged her stepmother rightly. Food that should have been fairly shared among the family had mostly gone down her gullet, until she became a hefty seventeen stone, while Lizzie's younger sisters and brother became thin as matchsticks. The two little girls died of consumption, the brother developed a bad cough, and the father – perhaps no longer wanting to live – just died to get away from his problems. He left two dwellings which he'd inherited: the cottage he lived in and the smaller one next door. One was left to Lizzie, and one to her brother, who became our grandfather.

Lizzie paid for, and attended, her father's funeral. Afterwards she promptly turned her stepmother out, and decided to make a home for her brother and look after him in a way he'd never known. It was no good wasting love on the dead, but she had an abundance for her little brother.

The cottages were in poor repair and seemed like hovels to Lizzie coming from the manor house. She enquired around for the cheapest skilled labour to do the repairs. She did the unskilled labouring herself. She mixed mortar and wheeled it in by the barrow-load; she fetched and carried in the role of builder's mate, till her hands bled and it was agony to straighten her back. The builder reckoned it was the hardest money he'd ever earned, keeping up with her. When the building was finished, she still had enough money left to buy some bedsteads; she intended to earn her living by catering for lodgers.

She took in three middle-aged miners – a widower and two surly bachelors. Lizzie fed them well, did their washing, kept the cottage spotless, and expected (and got) their weekly board money each Friday on the dot. She paid twopence a week for her brother to learn to read and write at a dame-school in the village, just as her father had paid for her before she left home. And she started to dig the garden, but her lodgers took the spade from her hands. Lizzie's rabbit pie, meat dumplings and treacle roly-poly were well worth a bit of digging. When, at the age of eighteen, she took and married the fifty-year-old widower, nobody was surprised. She was considered staid and mature far beyond her years.

Now he shared her bed, Lizzie could take in another lodger. This was a gentle bachelor, John Webb, a safetyman in the pit. His kindness helped her when, at the age of twenty-three, she was widowed by a pit-fall. Five years later, John Webb summoned up the courage to propose marriage to her.

She loved John Webb with all her heart and fretted that she could not bear him a child. She grew quite beautiful; and, in her old age, she would often recall the day they went to Speech House fair. She wore a pale-green silk bustle dress, with parasol to match. She pinned extra side-curls to her own abundant brown ones under her Dolly Varden hat. 'It had a wide pale-green ribbon to match, and a big pink rose in every dip in the brim. Lady Webb, they called me, after that day; and John held my arm and walked me about as though I were the Queen herself.'

When he was twenty-one Lizzie's brother married, and settled down in his cottage next door. Now he was off her hands, and with little to hinder them and a tidy nest-egg of golden sovereigns, John and Lizzie decided to sail to America and seek their fortune. It was the time of the California Gold Rush. Lizzie was too prudent to sell her cottage. She gave notice to her lodgers and let it.

Off they went, sailing steerage class from Southampton, and then travelling across America by covered wagon, till they reached California and a gold-crazed miners' camp. Gold there might be, thought Lizzie, and again there might not. But men needed feeding and housing. Let John try for the gold; she would ensure their living by running a boarding-house. She chose only the more respectable types for her lodgers, and her venture prospered well enough to make up for John's practically barren claim.

Lizzie picked some gigantic oak and chestnut leaves, and put them between the pages of her enormous family Bible. Some day, when she returned to England, her friends would marvel at them. That day came sooner than she had dreamed. John Webb had never been robust: now his pallor had turned to yellow, and he lost his appetite. A doctor diagnosed cancer, far advanced. It was unthinkable to Lizzie that John should be buried in foreign soil; she was not sure that the Almighty had stretched his jurisdiction as far as America. She sold the boarding-house, booked a more comfortable passage home, for John's sake, and brought him home to die. They'd been away two years, and she was now almost penniless. So once again she earned a living taking in lodgers.

Her brother still lived next door and like her was, in the local idiom, 'a reg'lar scrat'. He did all available hours in the pit, kept a few sheep and pigs, and was always at the ready to earn a few coppers extra if the chance came his way. Somehow he was always finding the time to enlarge his cottage. He was now the proud father of a baby son, and wanted to become a man of property. But his frantic, tireless striving had taken toll of his doubtful health. All Lizzie's efforts at building him up had been dissipated by overwork. She became very worried about his cough and his thinness, but he was a married man now, and no longer her beloved responsibility.

Gathering acorns for his pigs' winter feed, he went into the forest in pouring rain, and caught a chill which flared into pneumonia. In less than a week he lay dying. 'Kip a eye on me little boy,' he said to Lizzie. He loved his young wife very dearly, but regarded her as a feckless young girl compared with his practical sister. Lizzie would have taken the baby to bring up as her own, but the young mother wouldn't part with him altogether. Instead, she took her baby son home for her parents to mind, let the cottage at one-and-sixpence a week, and herself went back into service, to earn her keep and his. This baby, Charles, was to be my father.

After three years she married again, another miner, and came back to her cottage. There she gave birth to eight more children; and Great-Aunt Lizzie was three-quarters mother to Dad and half-mother to the rest of them.

As he grew up, my father Charlie became her idol. He was impractical, dreamy, clever, and utterly kind. There grew between them a bond of affection such as I have never seen. She forgave him his wild atheistic talk for she knew he wouldn't hurt a fly. She forgave him his foolishness in marrying a Welsh girl she couldn't really like, because he had the needs of a man. He'd gone to work in the Welsh coal-fields because of the slump at home. When he married, Lizzie let her cottage again, and went to join him in Wales, where she rented a cottage to share with him and his new wife. Soon there was a beautiful baby girl named Elizabeth – my sister Bess.

When the slump hit the Welsh coal-fields, they all came back again and settled in Great-Aunt's cottage. Though seven more children were born, it was unthinkable that we should move. Over the years we broke most of her treasured china and ornaments. On Sunday afternoons her red plush cloth was put on the table, and we little ones sat underneath and pulled the bobbles off. When she was still able to get upstairs to bed, one or the other of us warmed her old bones at night.

One thing we were not allowed to put our mischievous hands on was her best hat. It was a big-brimmed black straw. I don't know what trimmings it had started out with, but over the years Great-Aunt had sewn on to it every black trimming that came her way. There was an ostrich feather, cartwheels of black tulle, bits of lace with jet beads, rosettes, bows of black ribbon, bunches of black cherries and a bird or two. Sacred, nebulous, amorphous, it resided in its own special cardboard box, to be brought out and worn for the significant occasion.

One such was a chapel anniversary at which I recited a poem. Despite her crippling arthritis, she decided to come. Dad was no chapel-goer, but he gave her his arm; and with her walking-stick in her other hand, and allowing an hour for a three-minute journey, they made it. She was so pleased with my performance, that she gave me the honour of carrying her hat to her room afterwards. I laid it carefully on the bed.

Despite Mam's efforts, we always had fleas, but that summer we were infested. They were torture to Great-Aunt Lizzie; for by the time she had reached one bite to give it a good scratch, 'the tarnation critter' would bite somewhere else. She bought boxes of Keating's powder to sprinkle under the feather beds, and in the patchwork quilts. It made us sneeze, and itch worse than the fleas. She used to blame the cat for the fleas, for she was always catching him on her bed.

After the efforts of the day she decided to go to bed early. But soon she was back; she opened the kitchen door and stood there forlornly holding a battered black object.

'Me 'at! Oh, me 'at! I thought as 'twere that dratted cat on me bed, so I gi'ed 'im a whack wi' me stick. The pestering critter never budged. I'll teach him for once and all, I thought. So I really laid into 'im wi' me stick summat cruel. No wonder 'im didn't muv. 'Twere me 'at I was whackin'.'

The sight of that bedraggled hat with the ostrich feather limp and broken, the birds moulting, the cherries plucked, the bows undone, the roses picked, was too much for Dad. He just had to laugh, and it set us all off. She even forgave him for that.

'Never mind, Auntie,' my sister soothed her when she got her breath back, 'I'll mend it for you so no one'll notice, even if it takes me a week.'

We all knew how clever my sister was. 'All right, my wench; and it'll be doing you a good turn too, for I be leaving you that 'at in me will.'

I'm not telling anyone what my sister said about that, behind Auntie's back of course. Sure enough, though, she did wonders to restore that hat, but poor old Auntie was never again well enough to go out in it.

# Granny and Grancher

Until I was about ten years old, Granny, Dad's mother, lived in the cottage next door with her second husband, Grancher. Like our Dad, Grancher was a miner, dour, handsome, uncommunicative. Granny bore him seven daughters, and he greeted the news of each birth with a resigned grunt and a spit into the back of the fire.

But Granny kept her trump card under her pinny until the last moment of her child-bearing years. Then, belatedly, she presented him with a baby son. Mam said Grancher nearly fainted when he was told, and that Grancher went upstairs and kissed Granny and his little son.

He nearly turned into an ordinary human being after that.

In some ways, we were lucky to have such a grancher; he never gave us a cuff round the earhole, or shouted at us. But we were aware of his prickles, like a hedgehog, and even as toddlers developed a sort of radar to avoid contact with his chair or person. His wooden chair was the only one with arms on, and it was sacred to his use. In the winter, when there was no gardening to be done, and not much work in the pit, Grancher dozed away the time by the fire chewing his cud of twisted tobacco.

Lively Granny would be off into our house for a quat and a chat; and then we children used her place as a play house. So long as we didn't kick into the rungs of his chair, or make physical contact with him, Grancher completely ignored us, and would not have turned round if we had been walking upside down on the ceiling.

When any of my aunties came home from domestic service in the winter, they used him as a clothes airer for the stockings and blouses they wore for meeting their local beaux.

One autumn I sat for three weeks, after school hours, on Granny's steel fender, 'atching out a cuckoo!', and I don't think Grancher noticed I was there. This was a ploy my sister thought up to get rid of 'our little misery guts', as she called me.

'See this 'ere fir cone,' she said to me in her special confidential whisper, 'well, that's where the cuckoos do come from. That pink down there in the spikes is the blood. Now if you do sit on Granny's fender, an' kip a-turning this fir cone round by the fire, a dear little cuckoo'll 'atch out. But don't tell anybody what you be doin', or the spell'll break.'

So there I sat.

Luckily for me somebody in the village killed a pig, and gave Granny the chitterlings. These had to be cleaned in a zinc bath on the table, for we had no sinks, taps, or running water. The smell drove Grancher out; he must have found a couple of pennies to go down to the pub with. Granny's sense of smell was almost nil, due to a severe illness earlier on; but she kindly said 'that I might like to run out and play wi' t'others, till the wust o'smell was over.' I explained that I couldn't. It didn't matter about telling Granny our secrets; she was like father, and did not pooh-pooh our ideas. *She* believed in miracles.

'Well, I never knowed that afore. You do live and learn summat every day,' said Granny. 'I s'pose young Lizzie told thee that?'

'Aye, Granny, 'er did.'

'Mm, I thought so.' Granny took the cone, and solemnly held it first to one ear, then the other. Sadly she shook her head. 'I be a-feared thee'lt never 'atch a cuckoo outa' thic 'un, 'im's addled. But still, thee doesn't wanna disappoint Lizzie; thee tell 'er thic cuckoo 'atched out all of a sudden and fled up the chimley afore thee cust cetch'n. I must say Lizzie's a sharp wench, 'er can 'atch a cuckoo outa' all sarts. Now, thee take some big taters from thic box in the back-kitchen, thee'lt find Lizzie an' t'others roasting taters at the back of old Ben's pig's cot.'

Granny never knocked down our childish illusions.

Granny's kitchen was as friendly to us children as our own, and the big fender round the hearth more familiar to my behind than any chair.

In the middle of the mantelpiece, the tea was kept in the Mazawattee tin, with its picture of a plump, bespectacled granny, and a little girl, the living spit of her, enjoying a cup of that famous brew. On each side were two other pretty tins. One, with a monocled dandy on it advertising Sharp's toffees, acted as filing cabinet for Granny's important papers; the other was her home safe, often rifled to find a spare ha'penny for one of us.

In the centre of the room was a big, scrubbed-top table, on another wall, a big chest of drawers. On the top of this chest was a photograph of a slim girl with her hair piled up in Edwardian style. Her tiny waist was accentuated by the fit of an ankle-length skirt, her close-fitting white blouse was high-necked, with leg-of-mutton sleeves. I thought the girl was quite beautiful, but I tried not to look at the picture too long in case Granny should notice, and start to think of Elsie.

Granny had produced some fine, handsome girls among her bevy of highly individual daughters, and if, at times, one seemed to have more imperfections than another, Granny still strove not 'to make poop o' one an' pudden o' another'.

Despite this, a stronger heartstring had attached her to Elsie; gentle, ladylike Elsie; delicate, difficult to rear, and treasured the more because of it.

With a natural aptitude for fine needlework, and a remarkable neatness in her own appearance, Elsie soon rose high in the ranks of domestic service. It was lucky, for she had little stamina to keep her going in the rougher, menial jobs.

The cough that had plagued her chesty childhood persisted, and one day Elsie just quietly fainted at her mistress's feet. The doctor was called, and advanced tuberculosis diagnosed. The servant was no longer worthy of her hire. Elsie was not the responsibility of her employers, and she was sent back home to 'recuperate'.

Granny was too familiar with the scourge of consumption not to be in great dread about her daughter. Up till then Granny had suffered much, humbly accepting 'Thy will be done', but she would not accept that it was the will of the Lord to take Elsie from her. He had blessed her with this special sibling, and Granny was willing to go to any trouble to save her.

A sofa-bed was made up for Elsie by the fire, and Granny became her round-the-clock vigilante; taking a day-time nap, when she could, on the bed upstairs, while Mam or a neighbour kept watch. At night Granny 'managed' with Grancher's chair, and another wooden one to put her feet up on.

'I'd be thankful if thee'st 'ould spare a bit o' thic for our Elsie.' With desperate candour, Granny asked for, and was willingly given, a share of any little delicacy that might find its way on to a neighbour's table. Elsie got the first pickings from the neighbours' gardens, the finest piece of liver from a new-killed pig, the best white meat from the breast of a sacrificed hen. All but Granny could see this bounty was in vain.

When the sun came out, Granny would pillow Grancher's chair, and carry her lightweight darling to the door. 'Is Mam's little wench feelin' better today?' On its thin stem of a neck the emaciated little face would nod brightly. Even when Elsie was too weak to pull the slipped shawl back round her own shoulders,

Granny clung on to her desperate illusion of hope. Everyone around her waited with apprehension for the end. They did not have long to wait. Against Granny's heart, the little bundle of bones, convulsed with her last blood-flecked cough, gave up the struggle.

''Twas terrible. We thought your Granny's reason was gone. 'Er sat that queer an' quiet, 'er might as well've been made out o' stone. 'Twas only days arter, when somebody said 'er reckoned the Almighty 'ad took Elsie to 'elp'n look arter all the little young uns they 'ad up there in 'eaven, 'er bein' such a good zart o' wench, that your Gran broke down and cried. Then we made 'er a nice cup o' 'ot tay, an' got 'er to yut a morsel o' vittles. But 'twere a long time before your Granny got herself right vut forrad agyun.'

Granny had never had the chance to learn to read or write, and she believed implicitly whatever she was told by religious Bible readers, whom she considered her betters by reason of their superior education.

But, education or no, in the year of the great drought she was generally credited with ending the water shortage. Rainless week had followed rainless week, and the spring that filled the well had died to a trickle. Women, children and men not at work queued for hours to fill a bucket.

Though by no means a finick about cleanliness, Granny did have her standards. Having turned her drawers inside out twice, in lieu of a change, she told Grancher that he must help her bring water from 'the splashes', as she *must* 'dab out a bit o' washin'. Going to 'the splashes' meant carrying a zinc bath half a mile, mostly down a very steep woodland slope, to a small valley stream that was still running.

Granny and Grancher struggled back up with the bath of water, seeking firm footholds, trying to hold the bath level, to take a rest, as there was no means of balancing it until they reached the top. Somehow they got home with most of the water in the bath, until they were negotiating the garden steps down to the cottage door. Right there, the handle came off Grancher's side, and every drop of water spilled out, mostly on Granny who was going down the steps first, and the rest over the tiny stone-flagged yard.

For a minute or two the shock of the cold water robbed Granny of the use of her tongue. Then, with a withering look skyward, she announced: 'If cleanliness be next to godliness, let 'Im see vit to send us down a drap more rain.'

During the night such an almighty thunderstorm blew up we thought the end of the world was coming. We hid our heads under the patchwork quilts, whilst torrents of rain found its way through every leaky cottage roof.

'I shall 'a' to be more polite 'ow I do ex fer things in the future,' said Granny.

Granny's voracious appetite for anything of interest that came her way made her as excited as any of us children when there was talk of a magic lantern show to be put on in the chapel. She always tried to find us a ha'penny, but not even her munificence could stretch to the tuppence each we needed as entrance fee to the magic lantern show. She suggested we might go and ask Mr Riley if he wanted some acorns picked up for his pigs. Mr Riley owned a fair-sized piece of ground by his cottage, and had turned it into a piggery. Letting the sows out to snuffle around for their own acorns was only possible if someone was there to see they didn't wander off.

Mr Riley supplied some big zinc buckets, and offered tuppence a bucketful. That year the oak trees had shed a poor crop, and it took a lot of scratching about in the sodden dead bracken and leaves to find the acorns. Oh dear, an acorn didn't go far to fill up the space in a bucket!

My sister had to have her eye on me all the time to keep me going. I was more interested in looking for the extra small and extra large acorn cups to make a doll's tea-set. Mam wasn't very pleased with me either, for the sodden leaf mould had soaked my boots, and rotted the uppers from the soles. With the bad economy of poverty, Mam had bought my nailed boots from 'Jacob's, the diddler'. He sold rock-bottom quality at rock-bottom prices. The thick 'leather' soles of my boots turned out to be compressed cardboard.

'Fat lot o'good,' Mam sniffed, 'spilin' sixpenn'orth o' shoe leather to earn tuppence.' We picked up five penn'orth altogether, and Granny made up the difference. Father mended my boots.

Come the great evening we were all set to go, Mam and the baby as well, but there was a bit of a hold-up with Granny's garters.

For everyday comfort Granny wore her stockings, slop-stocking fashion, rolled down round her ankles. Skirts were ankle-length, so it was no odds to anyone, but such informality could not do for chapel. 'Goo an' ex your mam if 'er 'a' got a bit o' 'lastic or string or summat, fer I can't lay me 'ands on nuthin' to kip me stockings up wi'.'

Mam frantically rummaged about for something, but had to call out that she couldn't find a bit o' nothin', not even if she wanted to hang herself with it. Granny wasn't beaten. She pantomimed to one of us to sneak the laces out of Grancher's boots, as he sat, apparently asleep, by the fire. It was a fearsome delicate job, but we managed it.

Although we were early, the front seats in chapel were already filled, and soon the place was packed. A stage had been improvised for the magic lantern show, and between it and the audience the chapel dignitaries waited with an air of importance. The audience waited, too; and waited and waited. The sniffs and coughs grew louder, but we sat stoically on. We'd paid our money: we expected results. One or other of the dignitaries kept going to the door on a fruitless errand to see if anyone was coming. At length one of them had to announce there must have been some sort of hold-up, and the show would be late.

Granny left her seat, and went over to whisper something to the young man who played the chapel piano. The next thing, he was thumping out *Little Brown Jug* and Granny was up on the steps, singing a lively rendering of it and dancing a cross between a sailor's hornpipe and an Irish jig.

She clapped her hands to the rhythm, and beckoned the audience to join in. Her choice of song in this temple of teetotalism caused the dignitaries to get a bit red in the face, but the audience loved it, and sang at the tops of their voices. Grancher's bootlaces didn't hold up, but who cared? Other impromptu turns followed, and by then I'd caught the mood of the evening. My exhibitionist tendencies came to the boil. Bubbling up and down on my seat, I shouted out, 'I wanna sing a song, I wanna sing a song!' And someone came to lift me up on the stage. Mam tried to pull me back. 'You can't go up on that stage. They'll be able to see your britches, and they be the colour o' the turnpike road where you bin playing on the ashmix.'

She was too late; I was up there. Anyway, at five years old the state of my drawers meant nothing to me. I only knew two songs right through – *Twinkle Twinkle Little Star* and a lewd, comical ballad taught me by a fun-loving auntie. The innuendoes, Greek to me, were ripe and fruity. My auntie had shown me just the right moments to ogle my eyes, shake where my hips would grow, and stamp my feet. I stood up there and let them have it. It brought the house down. The audience stamped, clapped and hollered for more. They threw halfpennies, pennies, and even a silver threepenny bit on to the stage. Quick as a monkey, I scrabbled up the money and, holding out a fistful, shouted proudly to my mother: 'Look, Mam, we shan't 'a' to 'ide in the back-kitchen from the baker, Saturday. I got enough money to pay 'im.'

Poor minister! Worried by such goings on in the chapel, he feared the house really would come tumbling down about our blasphemous heads. So he tried to put things right by mounting the pulpit, and getting the audience singing some well-loved hymns.

The evening ended in a mellow glow. Nobody asked for their money back, so all felt virtuous for contributing to the chapel funds. An old neighbour about summed it up when she observed to Granny: 'Well, s'welp me gawd, Liz, I enjoyed meself that much I'd forgot what I went there var in the fust place!'

When Granny and Grancher moved to another village we seemed much poorer, although we were actually two shillings and fourpence a week better off – that was the rent Dad let her cottage for. It had belonged to Dad's father, and when Dad was twenty-one it became his. He married at twenty-one, and he and Mam lived with old Auntie; but Granny thought he should have his own cottage, and told him she would find somewhere else to live, although she was still struggling with great hardship to bring up his brood of stepsisters. Dad wouldn't hear of it. 'It be thy 'ouse, Mother. I shall never make no claim on't; and I don't want it mentioned again, nor you ever to feel beholden to me for it.'

Thirteen years later, by their own scrimping, and with a loan from their daughters in service, Granny and Grancher were able to put down the money on a tiny cottage a few miles from where she was born. It was situated on a hillside, with a panoramic view of the beautiful Wye valley. Every day, till the end of her long life, Granny would stand and gaze long and gratefully at her riches.

When my father was killed in the pit (that was when I was thirty) Grancher and Granny were in their late seventies; but it wasn't his age that kept Grancher away from the funeral.

'I shan't come. I couldn't stand to see that good booy put under the ground.'

It was a lot for Grancher to say all in one go.

# The Doll

If the chapel treat was the highlight of our life in summer, Christmas was the pinnacle of our winter delight, though most of the joy was in the anticipation. Every year for many years I spent weeks getting excited about a hopeless dream. I wanted – oh how I wanted – a doll. I knew it was quite impossible for Mam and Dad to buy me one. I had no luck praying for one, and it wasn't any good asking Dad to put a word in for me in that quarter, because I'd heard him and his butties argue and come to the conclusion that there couldn't be a God, or at any rate not one who worried about us as individuals.

But Father Christmas was quite a likely benefactor, though he too had his limitations. *My* dad had explained to me that as Father Christmas was such an old man, with his long white beard, he couldn't be expected to carry big things for all the children. I should have to wait my turn for a doll. Meantime I must be satisfied with something small, like a penny box of beads, and an orange if I was lucky. My turn for a doll seemed a long time coming.

My patience ran out one autumn when I was nine years old. Gladys, my best friend, who already had a nice doll, was given the most fantastic doll you ever saw. I didn't begrudge Gladys anything – she let me nurse her doll, and dress and undress it. But that was like being a nanny, not the same as having your own baby. The new doll was the size of a child, had long hair, eyes that opened and shut, and wore socks and shoes. Gladys's dad had won it at Barton fair. The doll was much too grand to play with, and was put on display in their cottage. All the village children, and quite a few grown-ups, called at Gladys's home for the privilege of seeing it.

As far as I was concerned, matters regarding a doll had now come to a head. I couldn't help Father Christmas's decrepitude – he would *have* to bring me a doll this Christmas. I gave him plenty of warning by shouting my request up the chimney weeks in advance of the usual time. Towards Christmas I started to write notes to him as well, with a stub of pencil given me by a neighbour as payment for running errands.

I was puzzling out how best to put my case to him with the limited spelling and vocabulary of a nine-year-old, when Dad came in. I told him I was making a bargain with Father Christmas: providing he brought me a doll this time, he needn't bring me anything else ever. But it had to be a doll big enough to sit on my lap, and have hair, and eyes that opened and shut.

'I be a-feared 'tis no good thee exing Feyther Christmas for that sart o' doll, my wench. 'Im do only take that sart to the rich people's young uns,' Dad warned me kindly.

'You do want to tell the silly old bugger off then. Tell 'im they rich people can afford to buy dolls for their children. It's the likes o' we lot 'im do want to bring the best toys to. Why ever 'aven't 'im got more sense than that?'

Father, who usually had an explanation for everything under the sun, scratched his head and admitted himself 'proper flummoxed'.

Bess said I'd be lucky to get anything if Father Christmas overheard me calling him a silly old bugger. Just because she was gone thirteen years old, and would soon be going into domestic service, she fancied herself too grown-up to ask Father Christmas for anything. Anyway, then she would be rich enough to buy anything she wanted, for my auntie in Bristol was getting her a job with the fantastic wage of five shillings a week.

With hope only slightly diminished, I continued to shout my order up the chimney, and to send up my notes when the draught was strong enough to stop them falling back into the fire.

My little brother fell asleep on Christmas Eve long before I did. I kept poking him awake to keep me company, but it was no good. I must have been awake for hours, when I heard stealthy footsteps coming up the stairs. It must be Father Christmas! Should I look, or shouldn't I? I had the patchwork quilt pulled right up to my eyes – he wouldn't notice, if I just took a peep. I suddenly felt terrified.

It was a bit of an anticlimax when I saw my sister in the doorway! 'Oh gawd! I thought you was Feyther Christmas!' It seemed to me that she was hiding something behind her back.

'If thee doosn't go to sleep Feyther Christmas wunt come at all,' she scolded me.

'I can't,' I wailed, 'thee'lt 'a' to 'it I over the yud wi' the coal 'ammer.'

I banged my obstinate head into the bolster. 'Go to sleep, you silly little bitch,' I told myself crossly.

It was my excited little brother who poked *me* awake in the morning. 'Look – Feyther Christmas a' brought I a tin whistle, a orange, a bag o' marbles an' some sweets.'

I sat bolt upright, like a jack-in-the-box. My doll, my doll! Had Father Christmas brought my doll?

At the bottom of my piece of the bed was propped the ugliest apology for a doll one could ever hope not to see.

It looked for all the world like an old, darned, black woollen stocking, lumpily stuffed, with a bit of old ribbon tied tightly round the foot to form its head. The eyes were two odd-sized buttons, and it grimaced from ear to ear with a red woollen gash of a mouth.

After all that cajoling up the chimney, after all the notes I'd written, fancy him bringing me a thing like that! He must think me a horrible little girl to treat me so, but I couldn't be that horrible! Mam came in, looking a bit anxious, but she said, bright enough, 'Well then, Feyther Christmas didn't forget. 'Im did bring a doll for you.'

'Yes, an' 'im can 'ave the bugger back.'

Mother looked crestfallen. 'It won't break, like one o' they china dolls.'

'It's ugly, an' boss-eyed, an' got no 'air, and 'ow would you like it if the angels sent you a babby as ugly as *that*?'

Then I pulled the quilt over my head, to show I had cut myself off from the season of goodwill, and everyone concerned with it.

But Mam hadn't. After a bit she came back and sat on the bed. She didn't say anything, and my curiosity soon overcame me enough to have a peep at what she was up to.

Her baby boy, born a year after my little brother, had died; I thought he'd gone to heaven to be pampered and fussed over by the angels. Mam had kept a few of his baby clothes, though in general the women in our part of the village pooled their baby clothes to help each other out. Now she was dressing my doll up in a flannel nightdress, a bonnet and a piece of shawl. Held up in Mam's arms and cuddled against her neck, it looked like a real infant from the back. I was tempted to be won round. Mam left it, all snugly wrapped up, on the bed, while she went to get breakfast.

I and the doll were soon downstairs with the rest of the family, sitting at the table. Mam was in a specially good humour with me. We didn't have such things as bacon and eggs even on Christmas Day, but as a great treat old Auntie had given us half a tin of Nestlé's milk to share out on our toast. As if that were not enough, she'd given us each a shiny new penny as well. I felt warmed and loved again. I made a bit of sop in a saucer, with a drop of my tea and a bit of the bread and milk, and pretended to spoon it into my doll's mouth, before taking her out.

I knew that other children might laugh at her ugliness as they did at Lil Wills's poor little looney sister, so I decided to take her for a walk on my own. Miss Phillips, whose cottage garden adjoined ours, was just coming back from the ashmix with an empty bucket.

'My, my, Polly!' It looks as though Feyther Christmas 'a' brought you a real big doll this time. Let me 'ave a look at 'er.'

I loved the inside of Miss Phillips' neat, tidy cottage, but none of us were much taken with her – she nagged us for playing noisily, and wouldn't let us play ball where we wanted to. I gave her one of my ferocious scowls to put her off, but she insisted on following me and unwrapping the piece of shawl to see what I'd got.

'Oh my gawd, that'un 'ould do better to frighten the birds off the gyarden. I reckon Feyther Christmas musta took 'im from a crow's nest.'

How dare she? I bridled like an insulted mother! I doubled my scowl, and threw in my monkey face for good measure.

'Never mind,' I said to the doll, when we were out of earshot. ''Er's a nasty old bisom, and your mammy 'ouldn't change you for all the money in the world.'

Miss Phillips' insults cemented my feeling for my new charge. From then, she became the object of my affection.

I had taken squatter's rights of the narrow space between Dad's shed at the bottom of our garden, and the old stone wall of Miss Phillips' garden. Here I played whenever I could. Only my little brother, baby sister and my best friend, Gladys, were allowed to come in without special permission.

One hot, humid summer evening I was minding the two little ones down there, whilst Mam was doing some washing, when an ominous rumble growled across the sky, which had suddenly gone very dark. Almost simultaneously came a vivid flash of lightning that made my little brother jump. Mam had a morbid fear of thunderstorms: she screamed from the doorway for us to come indoors at once. I picked up my toddler sister and shouted at my brother to hurry; we got indoors just as the rain started to come down in a torrent. Mam took us to the coal hole under the stairs. Even here the tiny back window let in the lightning flashes, and the thunder seemed to be concentrating on knocking our cottage down.

Then I remembered! 'Me doll, me doll! I've left her down the bottom of the garden!'

Mother promised me she would be all right, and when the storm was over she would dry her out on the fender. The storm lasted past our bedtime, and though the rumbles got quieter and there weren't so many lightning flashes, Mam wouldn't let me put my nose outside the door.

She promised that Dad would fetch the doll in when he came home from his late shift at the pit. In the morning there was no doll on the fender when I got up. Mam had forgotten, but she ran down to get it before I could put my boots on. She came back with the disintegrating remains.

'Bain't no good you carrying on: it fell to pieces in me 'and.'

Despite a halfpenny and a few currants in a piece of paper, I was still sniffing back the tears when Gladys came to call for me.

'Never mind, Poll,' she said. 'We'll give her a lovely funeral. I'll go back 'ome and ask Mam if we can 'ave some flowers to put on the grave.'

She came back with a bunch of sweet-williams and an old straw hat. ''Ere, you be the chief mourner, you can wear this.'

We decided to hold the funeral in private. My little brother would probably only cry, and there was no one else worthy of the honour of attending. Gladys spoke a long sermon, then walked round the grave three times chanting, 'Ashes to ashes, dust to dust, if Gawd won't 'ave her, the devil must.' Then she put a handful of earth on the remains, and we filled up the grave and put the flowers in a jam jar on the top.

'O' course the devil *won't* 'ave 'er,' said Gladys.

It was nice of her to say that, but I never had a doubt where my beloved doll would go.

# 1926

No matter how crowded, it was a rare cottage where the occupants did not squeeze up to find room for the cripple, the simpleton, or even the 'bad penny', seeking the solace of companionship round somebody else's fireside.

When it was time to die, the good doctor had to let ill alone. As long as old Foresters could crawl to the chair by the fireside, they did so – poking the fire to life not just for the warmth and comfort, but to see their young days dance again in the flames. When the time came to give up the ghost, they prayed to do it in their own beds. They dreaded being taken to the workhouse – a brick and mortar reality – more than they dreaded the thought of the hell fire they had only heard of.

I once went to visit a dying old man, taken in mercy to the hospital from his neglected hovel of a cottage. Still alive, after the shock of an all-over bath, a pedicure, a manicure, and a fresh white bed-shirt, he lay between snowy sheets in the warm comfort of the bright ward, waited on by kindly starched nurses, but I could read the desperate message in his eyes before he struggled to gasp out the words, 'Please take I wum to die!'

Unless they slipped away without warning, there was never a shortage of sitters for the vigil hours of dying. When it was a child, hands were wrung, tears coursed down cheeks, and the sighs were strong enough to bear the little dead spirit to its rest without a wind from Heaven.

Poor Tilly Toomey was forced to bed a fortnight before the end. Despite a rota of bedtime sittings from her neighbours, there were times when Tom, her husband, had to take a turn. Tom Toomey had never been reckoned a patient sort of man.

'I bin a good wife to thee, ain't I, Tom?'

'Aye, that thee 'ast, Till.'

'I brought up thee young 'uns the Lord spared us as best I could, didn't I, Tom?'

'Aye, aye, my wench, thee didst.'

'I allus tried to 'ave zom vittles o' zom zart on the table when thee'st come wum from pit, didn't I, Tom?'

'Yus, yus, thee didst.'

'An' I allus tried to 'ave a clane shirt putt by for thee for funerals, didn't I, Tom? There's one in the top drawer, ironed ready, but thee must air'n a bit to wear for I.'

'Aye, aye, all right, 'oman.'

'An' I tried not to oversalt the bacon when I cured the pigs, didn't I, Tom?'

'Aye, aye, that's all right enuff, Till – but do stop thee frettin' about they things now. Thee save thee strength to get on wi' thee dyin'!'

Unless it was a matter of life and death the doctor was not called to our house – we were ages behind with the quarterly five shillings he charged for his services. In dire necessity a shilling or two would be scraped up from somewhere to get him to call, and he never let anyone down, God bless him.

Mostly our Dad cured us with his home-made potions. He gathered elderflower, yarrow, camomile, and other wild herbs, dried them and stored them in brown paper bags for his bitter brews. Constipation, coughs, colic, sickness, diarrhoea, sores, fever, delirium – whatever we had, out came the dreaded brown jug, and on the hob it went with its infusion of herbs. No matter how ill I was feeling, I used to feel I would rather die than drink that brown liquid horror. Death was at least an unknown quantity: the taste of Dad's herb tea was not. Vicious as a polecat, I would screw myself up into the wooden armchair and battle would begin. Dad rounded up his helpers – Granny from next door, Mrs Skinner from the other side, Mam, and old Great-Aunt Lizzie, who was too crippled to do much except her share of the scolding. A clothes peg was fixed on my nose.

'Now 'er'll 'a to open 'er chops,' said Dad. 'You 'old 'er arm Mrs Skinner. You, mother, 'old t'other. I'll 'old 'er yud still, and when she do open 'er chops to breathe, you get a good dose down 'er gullet. If we can get it down 'er, and 'er to bed for a good sweat, 'er'll be right as ninepence in a day or two.'

Desperation gave me superhuman strength. Somehow I would twist my head aside just as Granny was about to pour. Eventually some of it would find its target, but what Granny could get down, I could bring back up.

'Well!' gasped Mrs Skinner, 'I don't know about getting 'er in a sweat. It's brought us lot out in one!' She mopped her forehead with a corner of her sack apron. 'They do say it's good 'uns the

Lord do take first, so I don't see why we be bothering to drench that varmint.'

I was put to bed in disgrace, but Mam made me some toast tea. We were sometimes lucky enough to get an orange at Christmas, but lemons were a luxury we never saw. For feverish sore throats Mam toasted a piece of bread to near blackness, put it in a jug and then poured boiling water over it. When cool, this rather acrid drink was strangely refreshing to a parched throat.

All of this happened in its usual sequence when I was twelve and got scarlet fever. By the time the rash erupted and they guessed what was wrong with me, I was very ill and the doctor had to be sent for. Dad borrowed Mr Skinner's bike to help to do the two-mile journey quicker. On the way back, he made a long detour to the little town; then, before the doctor arrived, came rushing breathless up the stairs. From his pocket he pulled a thin oblong parcel wrapped in brown paper, unwrapped it, and showed me something I'd coveted without hope for years – a box of water-colours.

'There,' he said. 'Thee'll be able to paint to thee 'eart's content when thee'st do get back wum from thic hospital. See – Dad'll hide the box behind this picture so no one'll know about it. Now you hurry up an' get better, an' back home quick, for your old dad.'

I was sent to the Cottage Isolation Hospital, where I nearly died. But seven weeks later I tottered up our garden path on spindly, emaciated legs, 'a sorry sight for sore eyes', as Mrs Skinner put it.

My convalescence was not helped by the fact that the men were out on strike again – it was nineteen twenty-six. The strike was really a desperate cry for the status of manhood – to be able to do a full week's work in the pit, to be paid enough to fill the bellies of their families. The women stood four-square behind their struggling husbands, the older children sensed it would have been better if they hadn't been born, and apologised by being quiet and undemanding.

Some city people, mostly working-class and sympathetic to the miners' cause, offered to take miners' children into their homes to ease the burden for a while. One day two ladies came to our cottage and said one of us could go. As I was still terribly thin, it was decided to send me in a party going to London.

Mam was a dab hand at cadging anything that was going for her family, but she spoke no more than the truth when she told them I had nothing fit to wear to go in. From the pile of shoes and clothes collected by charity, they found me a dress and a pair of black boots. Both were brand-new! Alas! the boots were too narrow for my feet, broadened by wearing well-worn left-offs. A quart may not go into a pint pot, but my feet had to go into those boots. The cotton lock-knit dress was a narrow, shapeless tube in a hideous design like grey-black snakeskin. Luckily my tight boots only enabled me to mince along, so I couldn't come a cropper by taking a full stride in it. A neighbour contributed a hat. It had been a good one in its time, a brown velvet with a wide brim lined with green velvet. Someone had cut most of the brim off, and left a shaggy edge to prove it. The crown was on the big side – I had to wrinkle my forehead up to raise it for vision. Mrs Skinner, in a fit of generosity, gave me her cardigan. Mam cut off the frayed cuffs and hemmed them, and darned the holes. The shoulder seams came down to my elbows, and it reached long enough down to hide a lot of the dress. Nevertheless, a cardigan was considered a very modish item.

In full regalia, on the morning of my departure, I felt I was dressed to kill. It helped me to bear the torture of walking a mile in those boots. Mam came with me to where the party of children would board the char-à-banc for the journey to the station. The other twenty-four children had already arrived when we got there. The two ladies who were to be in charge of us for the journey to Paddington exchanged a meaning look when they saw me, and seeing the rest of the children, mostly little girls, I guessed why. My self-satisfaction ebbed away fast. They all seemed remarkably clean, and by our standards, dressed up to the nines. Some of them had little cases or cardboard boxes. Like aristocrats, almost imperceptibly, they left a little space each side of me in the char-à-banc.

I didn't care very much. I just withdrew into the delightful daydreams my imagination had conjured up for the outcome of the journey. I thought chiefly about my favourite page in my favourite comic, *The Rainbow*, which was about 'The Two Pickles', a curly-haired brother and sister who lived in a lovely house. They had a pet dog, Fluff; their father seemed to have plenty of money; their mother never got irritable like our Mam. Reading about the Pickles' mummy, I forgot that our Mam worked and worried over us all day, never had a new rag to her back, never went out for her own pleasure, and did her best against terrible odds. I took all she did for granted, but I noticed she wasn't often gentle and soft-tongued. I'd made up my mind that the lady who was going to have me in London was just like the Pickles' mummy.

My self-centred imagination pictured a house like theirs but without any Pickles – I was going to have her all to myself. She would buy me a pink silk dress, white shoes and socks, and call me 'darling' and 'dear'. We should eat off a proper table-cloth with lace round it, and have liver every day for dinner, and fancy slab cake for tea. Her husband would always have a pocketful of change, from which I would have frequent pennies for sweets. I dwelt so much on these fantasies that I came to believe in them. God knows my rose-coloured glasses had been knocked off enough times, but I never learned. Anyway, the fact that I was going to London was enough to make me believe in fairies.

London was the centre of the universe. Kings and scoundrels had hallowed her pavements with their tread. In the classroom London had seemed a world away. I'd never expected to go there in all my life. I knew I would feel a more important human being when I did.

It was a great surprise to find out how big England was: the train from Gloucester seemed to be going on for ever. One of the girls, called Florence, asked the lady escort in our carriage if perhaps the train had gone through London and forgotten to stop. By the way the lady laughed it appeared Florence had made a fool of herself. She didn't feel herself so much above me then, and began to talk to me. She was very tidy, but extremely plain – a droopy sort of girl, chinless, round-shouldered and very thin.

When we got to Paddington I couldn't see it. Like an insect to a man's hand, I couldn't recognise the whole object because of its size. The little bewildered tribe of us were shepherded into a sort of cattle pen. Outside it waited a lot of people, our prospective hosts. One by one the children were led out as people decided which of them to take into their homes. As the numbers thinned we huddled in the middle. Soon only two were left: Florence and me. 'O God, don't let me be last!' I prayed.

After a pause, Florence was taken out. But it seemed that the stomach of charity was not strong enough to take me. I hung my head in shame. I was not only unwanted, I was a nuisance. To make it worse, I couldn't hold back my tears. I wiped them away quickly with the sleeve of my cardigan. As I stood there alone, a thin young man with a very kind face and manner hurried up to me. 'Come on, kiddie,' he said, 'I know where we've got a nice home for you. Are you hungry?'

I shook my head: I'd never felt so full up.

Off we went. He took me to a large building in Westminster. On the way we passed Westminster Abbey. 'You must come and see it inside,' he said kindly. 'You may never have the chance again.' We went in, and I sensed his appreciation of its wonders by the way he gazed about. But I was too ignorant, and too worried about his problem of getting rid of me, to make the most of my chance.

I think the building we went to must have been Transport House. He took me up some stairs, and told me to sit in one of the big fat chairs in the most luxurious room I'd ever seen. It had huge windows. I looked out at the traffic, trying to regain my sense of reality. 'Shan't be long,' the young man promised, and went away, leaving the door open.

Presently a young lady walked by, and looked inside – looked again, harder – then came back with a couple more. Gradually a small crowd of people was hanging around the doorway. Some of the girls clucked their sympathy at the sight of me; some could hardly stifle their laughter. One kindly girl put a banana in my hand, another followed with a piece of chocolate. One came up with a bag of peanuts, while another tied a wide blue ribbon round my neck in a bow. They were well on the way to making a proper monkey out of me, but scuttled away guiltily when the young man came back and gave them an angry look.

'We've a nice home for you to go to in Kent,' he said, trying in his goodness of heart to give the impression I was someone special instead of something scorned; but he didn't fool me. I felt very tired, and I thought Kent was at Land's End and a further journey away than the one I'd already done. My big ideas about this adventure hung like a penance on my spirits. Just as well if I slipped off the edge when I get to Land's End, I thought.

We went to a railway station and into a restaurant, very palatial with potted palms and snowy table-cloths. We sat down, and he ordered himself a cup of coffee, and for me a glass of milk, a ham sandwich, an apple and a bun. He seemed quite at home in such magnificent surroundings. I was glad he took a newspaper out of his pocket to read, for I didn't feel at all at home. The ham sandwich was delicious; so was the milk. Four plates I thought – one for each item! I'd never seen an apple served on a plate before; the knife beside it seemed quite superfluous. I ate the apple, peel, core and all, of course; the bit of stalk took some chewing, but I felt it would have been rude to leave it on the shiny white plate. I couldn't manage the bun; but I was sure the young man would be hungry before we got to Kent, so I put it in my cardigan pocket for him.

Presently he peeped from behind his paper and saw that I'd finished, so we went out to get on our train. The journey was over in no time. We were now in a place called Plumstead, he told me.

He stepped out briskly. I hobbled along, trying not to hinder him; but my feet had swollen so badly inside the tight boots that walking was agony.

At last he stopped and knocked on the door of one of a long row of identical houses. A plump woman with a kind face opened it. 'I've brought you the miner's child you asked for,' he told her.

Her face fell at the sight of me. 'Oh dear! you've brought a girl. It was a boy we asked for. It's a bit difficult with the accommodation, you see.'

Perhaps it was the combination of my hangdog look at this response and the supplication in the young man's face that made her say, 'Oh well, now you're here you may as well stay. We'll manage somehow.'

A fervent 'Thank you' from my escort, and he was off like a shot before she changed her mind. I don't blame him. And God bless him, wherever he is.

My hosts, Mr and Mrs Couch, had two daughters and a son aged eleven, seven and thirteen. They were working-class people of very modest means. Mr Couch had a job at the Woolwich Arsenal. Their budget must have been stretched very thin to let me in, but these warm-hearted people made me feel the luxury of being welcome.

When bedtime came that first evening, Mrs Couch washed my feet, now bleeding and blistered from the tight boots. Her kind concern soothed my bruised spirits as much as the Zam Buk ointment soothed my feet.

I stayed with them for five months, and during that time other kindly people gave me clothes. The local children treated me as a novelty, but in the nicest possible way. It was a strange new world of bricks and pavements, of the luxury of going, for a penny, to the public baths for a weekly hairwash and bath, tasting new exotic foods like Yorkshire pudding and stewed prunes, and waiting with excited apprehension for the gas stove's pop when the tap was turned off under the kettle. It was a happy and interesting interlude.

When I got back home, plump, well-dressed, with a brand-new accent, my family marvelled at the change. It soon wore off, of course, and so did the accent and some of the extra weight, but it was a long time before I ceased to revel in the joy of being back – back home with my very own family and friends, back at school which I loved, and back in my beloved Forest again.

# A Death

Now I was back at school in Miss Hale's class, every day was a fresh delight. In the dreaded sewing lessons Miss Hale put me to paint pictures for the classroom wall – I had a little talent for drawing and painting. Tidily dressed, I even earned some respect from the boys. But it didn't last long.

Our Mam had been taken ill with something in her leg which swelled up angry red and shiny. The doctor ordered her into the new cottage hospital, recently built in the Forest, about three miles away. My sister left her job in service, and she now ran the household, with what little help she could cajole or bully out of undomesticated me.

Before breakfast I walked a quarter-mile to get two buckets of water from the well. Then we had tea, and I needed no persuasion to take a cup into our beloved old Great-Aunt Lizzie before I went to school.

One morning she seemed very tired as I tried to wake her for her tea. I slipped my arm round her shoulders to ease her up on her pillows. How well I knew every furrow of her dry parchment cheek, and stale-sweet fusty smell of her unwashed old age.

'Come on, Auntie. I'll be late for school.'

With great effort she opened her eyes. 'Ta, my little wench – I'll drink it later. I be so tired.'

I kissed her, shouted to Bess that Auntie would want another cup later, as she was too tired, and ran out to school.

On my way home at dinner-time I called in at the grocer's, on Bess's instructions, to get a loaf. I had to ask for it on tick. This always made me squirm inside, using my ingratiating, begging-for-credit manner. Once I was outside with the loaf achieved, I skipped for joy. Now I had the lovely long walk home in the dappled sunlight that filtered on to the woodland path through the great oak branches.

In a clearing, a little further on, a tall plateau of slag from a disused mine tempted me to run up it, among the golden gorse bushes that bloomed on its grey bulk. A rustle in the branches of a nearby oak made me look up to see a red squirrel, bushy tail fanned out behind him, nibbling at something between his paws. I wished he could come down and talk to me.

I forgot the time – a habit that frequently got me into trouble – and so trouble was what I expected when I saw Bess hurrying towards me. I ran to meet her, holding up the bread as a plea for mercy. Her face was tear-smudged, and her eyes red from crying. 'You'll have to go back to the shop and ask for some tay and sugar. Old Auntie's dead, and we'll have to have some in the house,' she sobbed.

She couldn't be! The thought that Auntie could never feel sunshine or shade, see colour, or hear sound again, was not to be borne. I judged death by my own standards, and didn't reason that Auntie rarely moved from the fire, and took ages to turn her dry old bones just to look through the window. We children had, for years, brought the world into her on the end of our prattling tongues; and the seasons' offerings, to put into jam jars of water, for her to bury her old nose in and say, 'My, they be purty flowers, and smell so scenty.'

Of late, I'd sat, quiet as a mouse, keeping her company when her mind wandered. She saw, and talked to, people from the past that were all round her, but invisible to me. When they were gone, she would feel lonely if there were nobody real in the room. We made up most of her world, and she was a dear and integral part of ours. She cherished and protected us in babyhood and early years, and as we grew older we cherished her.

'Go on,' said Bess, 'you'll have to get some tay an' sugar. It wun't be respectful to 'er if we can't put a cup of tay when they do come to see 'er laid out.'

I turned back, wrestling with this first attempt to understand death. Asking for tea and sugar on tick now seemed unimportant. Only when Mr White, the shopkeeper, vehemently shook his head, did I burst out crying. Auntie must not be disgraced! When I could speak through my sobbing, I told Mr White what had happened.

Life is full of surprises. 'That's different,' he said. 'I respected that old lady. She never asked for one penny of credit, not like *some* I could mention. If everyone was like her, only spent what they could afford, life would be better for the likes of me. Here, take this tay and sugar out of my respect. I shan't put it on the bill.'

When I got home, Mrs Protheroe and an old lady we knew as Granny James was there. Mrs Protheroe, efficient, kindly and helpful, had washed Auntie and dressed her in her laying-out clothes. Granny James had picked the finest flowers from her garden. She was now throwing out ingratiating hints for a keep-sake, eyeing, with a covetous glance, one of the few good pieces of Auntie's china we children hadn't broken. Granny James's cottage was a regular magpie's nest of china and pretty nick-nacks, mostly garnered on the excuse of 'something to remember the dear departed by'.

They'd brought out Auntie's bits of food. The sight of her sugar-basin, partly used-up tin of Nestlé's milk, and half-eaten small loaf, and the thought that now she would never eat them were so poignant, I felt desperate and lost. For the first time I couldn't run to Dad to put the world to rights. But he was there. He'd come home from early shift at the pit a few minutes after Auntie had died. Still in his pit clothes, he sat staring into space.

'Don't thee fret thyself, my boy,' said Mrs Protheroe. ''Er went as peaceful as a lamb, dear old soul. 'Er's in a better place now; of that I be sure.'

But her words couldn't reach him. I knelt down by him, waiting. At long last two tears – the first I'd ever seen on his face – rolled down his pit-blackened cheeks.

After the death of a villager, a service was held in their memory at the chapel, three Sundays later. I was surprised to see Dad getting himself as clean and tidy as possible to attend the service for Auntie. He never went to chapel, and indeed held the opinion that in general organised religion was the opium dealt out to the masses by the cynical few, to obtain for themselves their own heaven on this earth.

Father was my truth. Father was my yardstick to measure the world by. How could he go to chapel for something he didn't believe in?

''Tis a okard question, my wench. But you see, though thy old Auntie died, 'er be still living in people's minds – people who do think different than we. 'Tis to please them that did respect and love Auntie in their way that I be a-goin' to chapel.'

I don't remember thinking about death before Great-Aunt Lizzie died, and I was equally incurious about birth – retarded, you might say. If I *had* any curiosity about it, I expect it was damped by the taboo nature of the subject. Up to the age of eleven or twelve, waist to knees was unmentionable; later than that, it was neck to knees.

It was no wonder, really, that working-class mothers put the poison in for Nature where their daughters were concerned. After all, they were obliged to send them out into the world at the age of fourteen, with their bodies unprotected except by fear of men and God. And despite all the evidence Nature provides for the country child, it never occurred to me, or other children that I knew, to connect the two sexes with having babies.

When my sister came home on holiday from service at sixteen years old, she was charged with the delicate task of filling in this gap in my knowledge. I was then twelve.

Poor Mam got it in the neck from me, then. She was completely puzzled why I refused to speak to her, or even to Dad if I could help it. I cried most of the time and was sullen and dejected. She thought I was outgrowing my strength, and got me some iron medicine.

But before this, when I was ten years old, and my little sister was born, it did occur to me to wonder where the nurses *got* the babies to bring to the cottages. Sometimes it wasn't even a nurse, but only Mrs Protheroe, so she must have been in the secret, too. It was obviously something they kept to themselves. After pondering about it for days, the 'truth' suddenly hit me on the way home from school.

In my excitement, I forgot my task of collecting kindling from under the trees to light tomorrow's fire. Instead I sneaked in with an armful of old cabbage stumps that Mrs Skinner had thrown out on the ashmix, and these I thrust into the oven in the side of our old-fashioned range to dry. Mrs Skinner had come into our cottage for a 'quat and a chat', and to coo over the new baby, lying in Mam's lap by the fire.

'I do know where babbies come from, Mam,' I announced proudly.

Mam's face reddened. She began to poke the fire, and go into a fit of coughing. 'Go an' fetch the little 'uns indoors,' she gasped. But I was not to be put off from my moment of glory.

'Let me tell you first where babbies do come from,' and I stood my ground inside the door. 'Well,' I explained, indicating a large flat surface with my hand, 'there's the sky,' then indicating a lower surface, 'and there's the earth. Well, you see, the angels do come to the edge of the sky wi' the babbies an' 'and 'em down over to the nurses at the edge o' the world.'

I knew babies came from Heaven, for they were all 'little angels' when they arrived at the breast, although as soon as they could walk they became 'reg'lar little devils', 'aggravatin' tarments', and 'dirty little toe-rags'.

But before the women could comment on my theory, an acrid

smell of burnt cabbage issued from the oven. 'You lazy little slummock, you,' shouted Mam.

Handing the baby to Mrs Skinner, she pulled the stumps out of the oven and whacked them with much vigour but poor aim at my flying figure – down the garden path, over the gate, and out into the forest for some proper kindling wood.

I felt it was very poor thanks for such valuable information; but perhaps Mam was upset that I had shown up her ignorance about babies in front of Mrs Skinner.

# Scandal

Folk in our village were short of most things, but sex at least was a luxury not denied them, though someone is reputed to have said, 'It's too good for the poor.'

In spite of the care taken by the mothers of the village to instil virtue in their daughters, sometimes, now and again, a problem child would grow in our midst. Such a one was Lollie Blackman. In summer Lollie's main occupation was looking for lovers coupling in the tall green bracken. More than once she'd been chased for her intrusion by a furious, trouserless swain. Mothers threatened their children with good hidings if they went further than the garden gate to play with her; but I had no idea at the time why Lollie was so black-listed.

Although her own mother naturally saw her in a more kindly light, even she was glad to pack her off to service when she was thirteen. It was then generally forecast that Lollie would soon be home again with her belly full of more than good food. This didn't happen as soon as expected, but promising news reached us through her mother after very few weeks that Lollie had left her place in Cheltenham and gone to London.

She was rather a swarthy girl, with straight black hair, heavy black eyebrows, and sallow skin. A couple of years later, when she came home again, she had frizzy, buttercup-yellow hair, a pink-and-white complexion that must have taken a half-pound of make-up to achieve, her own eyebrows replaced by two thin, pencilled arches high on her forehead, and butterflies painted on the calves of her legs. Other, more natural, eyebrows were to shoot up much higher than Lollie's from the surprises she had in store for them.

Chapel was the last place anyone expected Lollie to turn up, but she did. She had decided 'to open our cake-'oles' with a preview of the outfits purloined from a string of mistresses. You could indeed have put a baker's basket of buns in the open mouths of the congregation as she swept in wearing a pale lilac chiffon tea-gown, with wide wing sleeves that reached the floor.

Slowly she undulated up to a seat in the front. Wafts of perfume stronger than high-church incense filled the tiny chapel. The preacher might just as well have gone home. He was an old-fashioned, ranting, Bible puncher. Usually the congregation thought the halfpenny they put in the collection well spent watching him 'work hisself into sic a lather 'e could have shaved his whiskers off wi' the froth on 'em'. But this Sunday he didn't get a look in.

'Pity thee'st warrn't at chapel today. Thee'st missed seeing Madam Butterfly,' a neighbour said to our Mam. The women regarded Lollie as a big joke, but they were soon laughing on the other side of their faces when their husbands began disappearing.

'I dunno where Tom be got to. 'Im went out to feed the pig a hour agoo, an' I an't see nothin' on 'im since.'

'Must be along o' my Ern, for 'im a' cleared off somewhere too.'

'And our 'Arry! I been a-waiting for 'im to vetch I a buckut o' wayter from the well this last half-hour.'

'That's funny. Ben offered to goo an' get I a bit o' kindlin' wood, an' I should think 'im's a-waiting for the tree to grow.'

'They be up in the wood, sat down, a-watching Lollie Blackman take 'er clothes off,' piped up a young bystander.

The wives moved off as one woman towards the wood, but they didn't creep up quietly enough. All they saw was the scuttling movements through the tall dense green bracken.

''Ere, I 'a' got thee a nice bundle o' vire wood,' said one of the men sheepishly to his wife a bit later.

'Oh, thee 'ast, 'ast thee? Well 'ere's a bit o' stick from me to go with it!' And his infuriated spouse whacked a piece of it across his buttocks.

Next day she was gossiping in a neighbour's cottage and the neighbour said, ''Asn't thee better pop up wum to see what they mon be up to? 'Im might be up in the wood again to see Lollie Blackman.'

'No fear. I 'ticed the varmint upstayers meself afore I come out, an' I've tied un to the bedpost.'

All the women now kept an eagle eye on their husbands' movements. 'I cawn't even go to crap wi'out exing 'er permission,' grumbled one of the poor wretches. Men left the use of the little bucket privies in the gardens for the women and children, themselves going out to the woods for their own calls of nature, to the 'manhole', as it was called – a large natural hollow where they kept an old spade.

Lollie didn't come home again for a long time. It was quite a sensation when a detective came to ask her mother for Lollie's address. He drew a genuine blank, for though Lollie often sent her Mam a parcel or a few shillings, she put no address in.

Then one fine day she just managed to stagger up the hill to her Mam's cottage in time to get into bed and give birth to a beautiful half-caste baby boy. During his birth Lollie entertained everybody within earshot with her opinions of men and of nature's method of reproduction, in words that would have raised a navvy's eyebrows. The advent of this little dark stranger brought a touch of cosmopolitan sophistication to our village. After a few weeks Lollie was off again, leaving the baby behind. Her mother's delight in this piccaninny grandchild must have added years to her life-span. As to the rest of us, the whole village doted on this little novelty of a child and made a regular mascot of him.

Lollie was an exception. The standard of morals among the village girls was very high. It was a rare thing for one of them to come home from service in trouble. If she did, she was forgiven. One more younger child had to sleep at the bottom of the bed to make room for her return, and the family food was shared out a little thinner.

Poor Sukie was a different kind of exception. She never got into service. She lived alone with her widowed mother, who kept her porter ale in the teapot, and kept having swigs 'o' cold tay' – no one was fooled by this.

Sukie's father had died in the asylum soon after she was born. Some reckoned his brain had been turned by sheer aggravation when his wife, in middle age, gave birth to yet another girl. They'd already had a brood of daughters, who'd all gone into service, or died, or married away from home.

Sukie went to school, but there was too much of a draught between her earholes for her to learn anything. She had a desk in the corner of the back row and slept through all the lessons, except when a pupil was ordered to prod her awake to stop her snoring. She attended school till she was twelve. After that she spent most of her time wandering about in the woods, sort of singing to herself. When she was hungry she gathered up a bundle of kindling wood and took it to someone's door. If they hadn't got a bit of bread or a cold potato to spare they might pull her a carrot or turnip from the garden.

Taking pity on her, the elderly widowed landlady of the village pub gave her a shilling a week and a daily meal to do some cleaning and scrubbing each day. Some days Sukie started down the hill and forgot where she was going, but someone was sure to notice and start her off down the right track again.

Alas, in the course of time Sukie began to emerge from her forest wanderings with her drawers in her hand.

'Come 'ere you silly wench,' the women would scold her gently, taking her into their back-kitchens to put the drawers on again. They put no evil construction to this habit of hers, until her obvious condition proclaimed it.

'Dirty, low-down skunk, whomever 'im is,' they said in disgust.

'If I could ketch un, I'd casterate the bugger wi' a red 'ot poker,' threatened her mother.

But none of the village men was in danger of being recognised as the child's father – it was such a poor, wizened little creature, it didn't look like anyone.

Sukie hadn't the sense, her mother was too fuddled with porter ale, and they lived too near starvation, to give the extra coddling such a poor starter needed. He just lay and cried weakly. Mam let me go and see him, because I liked simple Sukie a lot. I thought he looked much more like a monkey than the new babies brought to our house, but I was very upset when I heard he'd died. Mam told me Mrs Protheroe had brought him, not a nurse, so I gave that good lady a piece of my mind for taking him to poor Sukie instead of to our house where Mam would have looked after him properly.

After two more babies, the village matrons decided that Sukie was a moral danger. They had her put away in an Institution in Bristol. With no woods to wander in and with nobody to care whether she had her drawers on or not, poor Sukie soon pined away and died.

Before long two other misguided characters moved into the lime-light of our little stage. 'A bright pair o' beauties they two be!' the respectable housewives sniffed. I didn't consider Tilly Pudge and Minnie Meadows bright or beautiful, but they were a friendly, relaxed pair, always ready to pour a cup of tea for anyone who dropped in. Mind you, it didn't pay to accept if you were the fastidious sort. A dirty cup would be taken from a cluttered table, swilled out with a suggestion of water from the kettle on the hob, and wiped with the corner of a dirty sack apron. If there was any condensed milk left in the tin under its hovering flies, you got a bit, scraped out with a spoon that had probably been licked by the cat and a mongrel dog and a variety of bare-bottomed toddlers.

Minnie and Tilly lived in adjoining cottages, but were always in each other's places. With them, housework was an afterthought rather than a habit. They were too friendly by nature to be disliked, but were often gossiped about by more efficient housewives. At ten years old or so, I found the gossip enthralling but largely meaningless.

'I don't think as they've washed their curtains or rubbed a rag over their winders since they got married.'

'Just as well, if you ask me. I for one wouldn't want to see what goes on in *their* places.'

'I don't know why their old men puts up wi' such a pair of good-for-nothin's.'

(So far so good for 'Big-Ears', but then would come the sort of thing that continually baffled me in grown-up conversation.)

'Doosn't thee worry. They be good for *summat* and that's all some men do think about.'

'Judging by the looks o' their two men, thee bist right there: both on 'em be like skinned rabbits, thin enough to pull dru 'ole in a colander.'

'I've 'eard they be so mad at it, they do get down in broad daylight, 'avin it on the mat in front o' the vire.' Came a time when the 'two beauties' took a great fancy for going into the forest for kindling wood, a job that normally fell to the children's lot.

'Don't tell me they two 'ould bother to frizz their 'air, wash their vit, and put on a clane pinny just to vetch a bit o' virewood.'

'It's sticks they be arter all right, but not 'ooden ones. Mark my words, they'll be coming back one day wi' more than they bargained for, and serve 'em right, I'd say.'

'What say we go for a bit o' wood in the same direction and see what we canst ferret out?'

One night I woke suddenly in the small hours to hear Mam trying to rouse Dad – 'Wake up, wake up, you great cooten! I can hear a woman screamin' as though 'er's bein' murdered!'

I heard Dad bundling down the stairs as fast as he could go, moving clumsily in his half-asleep state. I didn't let Mam know that 'Big-Ears' was awake, but lay still as a mouse beside my little brother and sister, who slept soundly on. It wasn't long before I heard Dad come quietly back upstairs.

'*Was* it somebody bein' murdered?' said Mam.

'It might be a couple o' murders before the night's out, but I 'ouldn't lift a finger to stop it if it were.'

''Twas that pair o' beauties then, I'll warrant,' said Mam.

'Aye, thee bist right there, Mother.' I heard the iron bedstead groan as he got back into bed. 'Seems that their two men got wind o' their antics and instead o' goin' on to the late shift, they doubled back quiet in the wood and watched to see what they two 'ussies got up to. Sure enough, when the kids were asleep, them two sneaked out to get up to no good wi' a couple of men in the ferns. I reckon by the time Micah and Absy a' finished wi' their hides tonight they'll be too sore to lay about wi' anybody for a long time to come, an' serve 'em right.'

I couldn't make head nor tail of this rigmarole. Whatever was it the two beauties were out in the wood for instead of being nice and warm in bed? And why was Dad, the kindest-hearted man in the world, so nasty about them? The illogical behaviour of grown-ups was too puzzling to be worth worrying over. I snuggled down against my little brother's warm back and went to sleep.

# Going to Granny's

It was a Sunday, it was a lovely day, my brother and I both had tidy boots to our feet; and Mam's fine row of summer cabbages had all turned into firm big-headed specimens at the same time, with one among them a regular king.

'I'll tell you what, if you two'll be good young 'uns and weed they couple o' rows o' onions for me, you shall take a cabbage over to Granny and Grancher's, after dinner.'

Granny had been gone for many months, and we still missed her badly; but Mam drove a hard bargain. Weeding the garden was always a horrible job, but weeding onions was the horriblest. The weeds were so many, and the onion spikes were so like the spikes of the grass around them that had to be pulled out. But we had been over to Granny's before, so we decided it was worth it. 'Now mind where you be puttin' your feet,' warned Mam, and left us to it.

Now and again the gentle breeze wafted to us the smell of our Sunday meat cooking, promise of delight to come, with cabbage and taters.

We eyed the gooseberries still left on the bush for Mam to make a couple more tarts with, but decided they were too well placed in view of the window to risk a foray. 'Stick at it,' said Mam, coming up to empty a bucket of slops between the rows of taters.

'Stick at it,' I mimicked, softly, in disgust. Time went so slowly weeding onions. The birds in the trees seemed luckier and freer than we. They just swooped across the blue ceiling of the sky, with no one ordering *them* about!

Then it happened. A bee, perhaps overladen with pollen, paused to rest on my head. It got in a panic when it lost its foothold in my hair, and turned me into a jack-in-the-box sort of lunatic with its frustrated buzzing. I was sure to be stung, and I feared that out of all proportion to the pain it would cause. Rushing blindly about, screaming and beating myself about the head, I danced over the garden, not caring where I was putting my feet.

By the time Mam, Dad, and our neighbours had rushed down the garden to my aid, I had been brought to a halt. With my eyes shut for terror of the bee, I had run into the rope swing Dad had fixed up for us at the bottom of the garden. Stretched to its full length, it had brought me staggering back, caught in a rough rope noose. The bee had stopped buzzing.

'Doosn't worry, 'im's died,' said Dad, picking its remains carefully out of my hair.

''Er might 'ave 'ung 'erself on thic swing,' said Mam worriedly.

''Twas wuth a tanner to see 'er a-caperin' about; better'n they monkeys in the zoo any day,' laughed one of the neighbours.

'Yes, and our Mam can get a bloody monkey to weed 'er onions, as I shan't do 'em agyun,' I sniffed.

Although it was Sunday, which made my language doubly sinful, I got away with it. I was excused as being in a state of shock. Our neighbour brought in her jar of goose-grease for Mam to rub some in my sore neck. This, with the effect of a plate of Sunday dinner, quite cured it.

'Rub your shoes over, and wash your hands and faces, whilst I go and cut the cabbage,' ordered Mam. Out of the garden she came, with the biggest, finest specimen from the row.

As well as generosity, there was an element of show-off in the gesture. Mam and Grancher had been keen gardening rivals. Who could dig the first feed of new potatoes had been the main competition between them. Grancher was an old hand at the game, and he knew a dodge or two; Mam was green-fingered with a deep, inborn love for growing things.

The narrow, paved yard, running the length of our two cottages, was divided by a four-foot wall. Access to each doorway was by a narrow garden path that circumvented it. As far as I can remember, Grancher never crossed this demarcation line to see what Mam got up to in her garden. But she wasn't above looking round *his* garden for horticultural hints, after she had popped into Granny's for a bit of a squawk.

Come February, whilst Grancher was at work, Mam followed the horses, a shovel under her arm, and a bucket in each hand. She wheeled in barrow loads of leaf mould from the forest, and when we had a pig, the cleanings from her cot were like treasure trove to Mam.

The first day there was no frost in the ground, she would dig a trench, and fill the bottom with her rich compost, then a bit of earth, and then the potatoes, before covering them down with a lovingly patted top layer of earth.

''Tis the smell of all that muck they taters can't stand. That's why they do push up so quick, to get a breath o' fresh air,' was Father's diagnosis of their remarkably early germination.

If it looked like a frost, Mam covered them with twigs and bits of dried fern till the danger had passed. When Mam knew she had a good start, she would call across the garden to Grancher, in all innocence like, to ask him how his taters were comin' on. Grancher never gave her more than a grunt and a shrug, but they were enough for Mam to read the signs.

Come about Whitsun time, and Grancher would come to the wall, clear his throat loudly, and put a sample of his first diggings on the top. Out Mam would go and give fulsome praise to such an achievement, knowing that Grancher, apparently standing indifferent in his yard, was smirking with self-satisfaction.

'I 'aven't tried mine yet. I'll 'ave a dig at one later on,' Mam would say. We had seen her, gently, oh so gently, scraping away the soil under the haulm, and burrowing with her fingers to feel the size of hers. She would wait until he came out into next door's yard again, then put *her* offering on the wall. Grancher couldn't resist having a look. If Mam's were smaller he would grunt quite kindly over them; if they were bigger, he spat into the corner of his yard, and stumped up the steps to his garden.

'I'll bet Grancher 'ant got a cabbage like this in 'is gyarden, but don't you two tell'n I said so.'

As the crow flies it was about a mile and a half to Granny's. For us, up hill and down dale, it was nearer two and a half. Mam watched us from the gate until we started down the steep wooded hill that took us from her view. Negotiating the wavy little footpath at such an angle, carrying a big cabbage, proved a bit awkward. I decided it was big enough to make its own way with a rolling start from me. It kept leaving the path to get lodged in the ferns, or against the trunk of a tree. It looked a bit battered by the time it got to the bottom. Never mind, I stripped off the broken outside leaves, and left them as manna from heaven and a nice change of diet, for the insects teeming busily among the leaf mould.

It was lovely down in the narrow valley, watching the little stream we called 'the splashes', where Granny and Grancher had fetched the water. It bubbled clear and gently over the pebbles. On down, a bit out of our way, was a place where watercress grew. Should we get some for Granny? Yes, it would be a good idea, because afterwards we could take our boots off to wipe away the mud with some fern. Then if we had our boots off, we might as well take off our socks and paddle our feet in the water.

We didn't manage to get any watercress, but we got mud inside and outside our boots. 'My vit do veel all squelchy,' I said, as we started up the hill the other side.

'An' mine do,' said my brother.

'Never mind, our Mam wun't know, they'll be dry by the time we do get wum.' Coming through the leafy branches, the hot sun made ever-changing, lacy patterns on our bodies.

'Phew, I be as 'ot as a fresh 'osses turd. I be a-goin' to zit down,' and my brother, suiting action to words, chose a spot where a swirl of dead leaves had made a soft place among the fern at the side of the path. I was feeling a bit hot and bothered myself, handicapped as I was by the cabbage which seemed to be getting more heavy and awkward with every step.

'It's your turn to 'ave a go carrying the cabbage,' I told him tartly.

'Ben't my job to carry'n; you be the biggest, an' our Mam give 'im you to look arter, not me.'

'Snakes do live in dead leaves. You do want to watch out, you might get bit to dyuth lyin' there.'

A bit of danger, real or imaginary, *did* add some spice to life. We carried on to the top of the hill a bit quicker after that. Once on the flat, we soon found a good shady place to rest; on a carpet of moss big enough to stretch out on. This place, we reckoned, was half-way to Granny's.

'We shouldn't lie 'ere, really. This moss is fairy ground, by right.'

My brother took little notice of this; he wouldn't admit to believing in fairies. I wasn't quite wholly convinced myself, but I was always looking for signs of the little folk in the woods. A bit of self-persuasion, and a lot of imagination, helped.

After all, there were all those fairy tales, and pictures of fairies, in the books at school. Perhaps if we lay very quiet and pretended to be asleep, some fairies might come to look at us, like the Lilliputians did in *Gulliver's Travels*. After a few minutes, I felt something on my hand; was it a fairy? No, a careful peep only revealed a ladybird; perhaps the fairies had sent her to see what we were. They'd never come out now, with two giants about.

'Come on!' I poked my brother sharply in the ribs; he really was asleep!

It wasn't much further to walk to the edge of that piece of the Forest.

Now the really adventurous part of the walk lay before us; a big stretch of rough grassland, with a cottage dotted here and there.

Here, ferocious dogs might come bounding out to snarl, and threaten attack on the two strangers.

If the cantankerous old gander spotted us, he would bring his flock of wives to hiss warnings at us from the end of their out-stretched necks. There was also an old black-and-white billy goat; true, he was tethered, but more than likely he would break his tether just as we passed him, and chase us. There might also be a couple of children about, bigger than us; you could never be sure if they belonged to a friendly tribe. Luckily, there were mostly grown-ups about too; busy in the gardens, or just standing looking at the work to be done. In a last resort, these could be yelled to for help.

We emerged from our ordeal with nothing worse than slightly faster beating hearts, and some kindly nods from an old man leaning over a gate. Down over the bank, and we were on the main road, and only a few minutes from Granny's place.

The main road went steeply downward in a horseshoe bend to meet another road which led to the River Wye. We did not have to go many yards down the road before we took the little path leading to Grancher's garden gate. A steep bank sloped from the main road to the back of the cottage, which stood, snug from the worst of the winds, on a narrow plateau. It was fronted by a garden terraced with little dry-stone walls to stop it slipping down alto-gether into the sharp incline below.

The level ground extended to the gate, and to a bit of garden to the left of it. Here Grancher was busy, to our surprise, among a patch of flowers. We expected no enthusiastic welcome from Grancher, and were certainly not prepared to be beckoned over, and asked to tell: 'What d'ye think o' they, then?'

We had no words to express what we 'thought o' they'. 'They' were about twenty different species of dahlias, and each seemed incomparably beautiful until you looked at the next. Grancher's rough hands, embedded with pit dirt scars, knotty and gnarled with work, made a perfect foil for their loveliness as he cupped each bloom to show them to us.

Which was the best, the modest pale salmon one, blushing pinkly at her petal tips, or that purple majesty, the size of a tea-plate? Soft yellows, mauves and pinks, brilliant reds, proud as a rich sultan in his harem, Grancher showed off his beauties; and his hands trembled with the ecstasy of it all.

'Oh, Grancher! They be the best flowers I've ever seen!' And so they seemed.

We decided we would give the cabbage straight to Granny. Just then she came to the door. 'Hello, me butties, is Grancher showin' you 'is dailies, then? What a lovely day you've 'ad to come over! Just see the river from 'ere. There! What d'ye think o' that? Ben't it a beautiful sight? All they fields and trees, and ups and downs, for miles and miles.'

It truly was a fantastic sight, but wasted on two hungry little morons, who were much more excited by the view of the plate of fancy cakes on the table.

Even before she had moved from next door to us, Granny had sometimes been wealthy enough to buy off the baker seven fancy cakes for sixpence for Sunday tea. Like the dahlias they were all special, but there was one extra special, the cream slice, and that presented problems.

With the mad generosity of grown-ups, Granny always offered the plate of cakes to visitors first. In the case of my brother and me, it would be to the one who had finished their bread and jam first. Granny always gave us two pieces of bread and jam, and even offered us a third.

The bread and jam was delicious with a cup of hot, sweet tea. It was too good to gollop down, yet we had to keep a wary eye on each other. We sought a fine balance – to get full enjoyment out of the bread and jam, yet to finish it just in time to claim the cream slice. This particular Sunday the angels themselves seemed to be keeping a special watch over us. There were *two* cream slices on the plate.

When tea was over, Grancher turned his chair to the fireplace, cut himself a cud of his black twist tobacco, and picked up the *News of the World*. Grancher could read, and Granny could not, but when they were on their own, with a bit of cajoling from Granny, he would read her some of the juicy scandals. I expect Grancher could write as well, but I do not remember seeing him ever put a pen to paper. Correspondence was a problem for Granny. Whatever the contents of a letter she had to get it second-hand.

Perhaps the great highlights of their lives as they grew older were the occasional letters they received from America. Pride and heartache overwhelmed them when they talked of 'Our Olive'. Olive, the eldest daughter, had married a young man of property, and they had gone to America to seek their fortune. The young husband had gone over first, to find work, and somewhere to live. Their first baby, Nella, was six weeks old, when, two months later, Grancher escorted Olive and her baby to Portsmouth, so that she could sail to join her husband.

Not only Grancher, but anyone of any age who could read, was roped in to read Olive's letters for Granny, until she knew them all off by heart. A second daughter was born to Olive, and, as they grew, photographs of them were sent home.

'To think,' Granny would marvel, 'that we 'ave got two little American wenches for granddaughters! But, oh, I'd give me right arm jest to 'ave 'em sit on me lap for vive minutes. P'r'aps one day we will see 'em, f'r our Olive's husband be doin' well out there, an' when they can afford it, our Olive's goin' to come back to see us.'

Granny and Grancher kept this hope even to their deathbeds, but Olive never managed the journey home.

We had eaten our tea, we had viewed the landscape, we had admired Grancher's dahlias, and we would have liked to stay on. But Mam had told us not to be late, and it was time to go.

Granny told us to thank Mam for the cabbage, and gave us each a kiss and a piece of paper containing a bull's-eye and a clove sweet. Feeling very content, we pointed our noses towards home.

When we reached the main road we had a little conference. Should we retrace our steps the way we had come, or seek new adventures by going the long way home, all round the road? The possibility of seeing a horse-and-cart, some strange faces, perhaps even a car, decided us to go round by the road for a change.

Before long we had cause to be pleased with our decision, a chance to gaze over the hedge and take a long look at Liza Ward's donkey. This animal had a small claim to fame. His mistress ran a one-woman hire service with this donkey and a cart. To advertise her services, she had taken part in a carnival, dressing up the donkey's legs in two pairs of her open-legged calico drawers, with frills round the bottoms. To add to its ladylike appearance Liza had tied a wide ribbon round its neck, and trimmed the straw hat through which its ears poked, with a band of red roses.

A few derided her for 'makin' a numbskull out of a poor dumb animal', but most of the spectators thoroughly enjoyed the joke, and business boomed for Liza. We moved on a bit quick when Liza herself came out of her cottage.

We passed a few stragglers out for a Sunday walk, but did not see one horse-and-cart, let alone a car!

The ferocious animals that might have escaped from a zoo, and were lurking behind each cottage to pounce on us, never materialised. Still, we had a nice cool dabble in the horse's trough beside the road near Mirey Stock. Being Sunday, we could not watch the slag-filled carts crossing the bridge from Waterloo pit to the slag heap.

But look, danger *was* at hand! In a little clearing among the trees on our left, some gypsies had made a camp. Gypsy women were all right, when they came, laden with babies, to sell clothes pegs at the door, when Mam or Dad were about. But gypsy *men*, with their dark skins, squatting round a fire, whittling at sticks with shining sharp knives, they were a different breed altogether! Gypsies stole children, and sold them in faraway places; if they got hungry enough, they would even make a stew of you, and give your clothes to their children to wear! This was more adventure than we had bargained for. With fear to stoke our engines, we ran like the clappers to the other side of the road, and along the grass verge until our very breath gave out. Rather to our surprise, the gypsies had ignored us.

Now they were behind us, and the first houses of our village were in sight. The welcoming sight of Mam coming out to look for us gave us the energy to hurry up to her. We took our places, one each side of her skirts. She clucked at us like a broody hen in a coop away from her chicks, when they run too far from her feathers.

Though I loved our visits to Granny's, it would have been even nicer if she had still lived next door. She was that rare thing, an ally for ourselves among the grown-ups. We missed the extra refuge of her cottage. This loss was brought home to me most powerfully one Saturday in late November.

'Just my luck,' said Mam resignedly, 'your feyther's got a good wage this wik, so 'is pit boots 'ad to goo an' bust open agyun. They be past 'im bodgin' up any more an' I might as well try an' get a pair for you as well, for your'n ben't much better. It's a nice day so I'll take the little'uns wi' me. Now mind you do as I say whilst I be gone. Get they forks and knives clean till I can see my face in 'em. Kip a good fire goin', an' put some taters in the oven for supper when we've bin gone about an hour.'

'I'll mind the babby,' I offered. Mam loved her children, and on reflection, felt her youngest offspring would be safer with her, than left to the tender but absent-minded and inefficient care of a Peter Pan sort of daughter, who was old enough to have, but was sadly lacking in, 'a bit o' 'omanhood'. Bess was by now away from home, in service, and besides, there was no old auntie to keep an eye on things.

I didn't press the offer; I had exciting prospects in store.

Also I realised it might be a bit of a ploy on Mam's part, to take three small children. The town tradesmen could not afford to be sentimental, but the wistful eyes of children would sometimes get a bit extra dabbed on the scales.

Mam was only a little woman, and the big plaid Welsh shawl her mother had given her nearly enveloped her as well as the baby. She carried the baby in it, Welsh fashion, after the manner of the gypsies who carried their babies as they brought pegs to the door to sell. I think the warm body of a child must act as a recharging battery to the mother's body. Women seem to be able to carry children for distances long after one would expect them to drop from fatigue.

I felt a small sense of guilt, watching the little convoy go down the garden path. It was soon dispelled by the thought of the book, which I knew father had 'hidden' on the top shelf near the fireplace.

For once I had the house, the fire, and a book to read, all to myself!

I spread some newspapers on the table, tipped the contents of the kitchen drawer on to it, got the brickdust and rags from the back-kitchen, and gave our odd assortment of cutlery an enthusiastic, if not very thorough, rubbing over. I banked up the fire; lumps in the front, small at the back; then I stood up on a chair to reach down the book.

Very little printed matter that came into our house was censored from us, but obviously Dad had considered *Coffin Island and Other Stories* by Edgar Allan Poe, a little macabre for young readers. It had been printed like a thick magazine, with a lurid cover illustration of a skeleton hanging from a dead tree, near a church, on a moonlit night; and lurking in the shadows were weird, ghoulish creatures.

A bit scary, but nothing to worry about, with the lovely autumn sunshine streaming in through the window, and a cheerful fire to sit by. Not time to put the potatoes in the oven yet.

Feeling as lucky as a cat shut up in a dairy, I pulled my chair up to the fire, rested my feet on the steel fender, and plunged into my feast of horror.

Very soon I was both repelled and fascinated. I feared to go on reading, yet dared not stop. Even the dancing flames of the fire could bring no cheer to the black mood of every page, although they brought enough for my young eyes to read by. What kind of mind could the author of this horror have possessed? The warm entrails of a fresh-killed corpse could have been his inkwell.

Only when the flames began to flicker down, did I notice that the daylight had quietly gone. The window was no longer a frame for the sunlit garden and distant trees; it now framed the black mourning of the night.

Outside the reach of the fire the little room had grown dark. Fool, greedy fool! So anxious to settle down with my book, I had not had the forethought to bring the lamp in from the back-kitchen, to put a spare bucket of coal by the hearth in readiness for making up the fire. Nor had I fetched the potatoes from the box in the back-kitchen to go in the oven.

And now I couldn't! Not only Poe's murderers and corpses were gathering in our little dark back-kitchen, but all the witches and ogres from my own mind's store had joined them. They might even now be coming behind my chair, waiting to pounce; to put their claw-like talons round my throat.

Mam, Mam, hurry home Mam, before the flame from the fire dies down, and I am left in the black pit of darkness, and they can carry me away! If only Granny had not moved from next door, or the young couple who had taken the cottage had not gone out for the evening!

Somehow I must find the courage to lift the poker from the fender and break the last bits of black coal into more flames, but take care not to turn my head or take my eyes from the printed page to acknowledge 'them', who I could now sense were in the darkening corners.

In those days damp courses were uncommon, and our cottages were breeding grounds for cockroaches. Though, perodically, Mam attacked every crack and crevice with Keating's powder, Jeyes' fluid, and boiling soda water, she could not stay the infestation of these pests.

They never emerged in daylight, or by lamplight, and never came up to the bedrooms. But when the family were in bed, and all was dark, out they came, to forage up the walls, in the rag mats, and even across the clothes line on the ceiling. We children hated them, and would never come downstairs in the dark, unless Mam or Dad preceded us with a lighted candle. Mam made her wallpaper paste with a flour mix. Now as the cockroaches looked for sustenance, their movements made faint crackles behind the paper. Only, to me, it wasn't cockroaches; it was the stiff black cloaks of fearsome witches brushing against the wall.

All the time, the glow of the fire went down until there was barely enough to read by. Concentrating on the page was less horrific than allowing my mind to dwell on the lurking horrors, crowding now right up round my chair. The draught from under the back-kitchen door came straight from graves freshly opened by fiendish vandals; I could almost smell the bodies.

Old Auntie's corpse had been laid out in the little narrow room adjoining. Now her spirit knew all about my wicked sins. Now she knew how I had crouched down on the mat by the fire, slyly waiting to steal the remainder of the sodden chewed crust from my little brother's hand, while he lay asleep on her lap. Now she knew that I had dipped my finger in her sugar basin. All my bad deeds came to the surface of my memory. Perhaps old Auntie didn't love me any more, now that immortality had opened her eyes to my sins.

I dared not raise my eyes, for old Auntie's ghost would not lurk behind the chair, or in the corner. No, she would come white and wraithlike, and scold me with a forbidding skeletal finger, to my face.

The fire was almost out. Only Mam could save me now, and it seemed that Mam would never come. Never? Wasn't that the creak of the garden gate? Wasn't that sound the sound of voices? The dear, familiar tones of Mam and the little ones? Yet not till Mam's hand closed on the doorknob to enter, did I find the courage to move.

Dispirited by the high price of boots, tired out, with aching arms and painful varicosed legs, hungry, her patience tired by the weary whimpering of the little ones, Mam's misery flared into righteous anger, as I scurried to light the lamp and fill the coal bucket.

The dead fire, the oven empty of the warm, roast potatoes she had used to encourage the little ones as they soldiered on through the woods, the selfish thoughtlessness of a daughter old enough to know better – all this should have got me the sort of hiding I deserved, if Mam had found the strength to give it me.

But she was almost in tears. 'Whatever 'ave you bin doin'?' she wailed. Mam never read a book herself. Her own life was too full of conflicts and troubles, work and excitement. It was no use trying to explain. Abject with guilt, I now tried to help her.

'I'll tell you what you can do, you lazy hussy, you can go up to Joe Meek's an' ex'n to let me 'ave a shillin's worth o' meat. Tell'n I'll pay'n for it next Friday wi'out fail. Thanks to buying you some boots, which you don't deserve, as well as some for your feyther, there wasn't a penny left for any meat for tomorrow's dinner.'

The relief at being safe, and secure in Mam's unimaginative presence, receded sickeningly at the thought of this new threat. All the horrible fiends that had fled at Mam's homecoming would be waiting out there in the dark; darkness now made even more sinister by the shadows thrown by the light of the emerging moon.

With a boldness brought on by terror, I begged that my little brother should go with me. Such a heartless request, on top of my other shortcomings, nearly made Mam explode. 'Wasn't 'is poor little legs nearly droppin' off, as 'twas, from 'elpin' to carry 'ome my boots, and vittles for the likes o' me, too idle to get off my arse to keep a bit o' fire goin', let alone put a tater in the oven for their hungry bellies?' Shame on me!

Ashamed I was. I had no case to plead for mercy, no grounds to give Mam some defiant cheek to try and dodge the errand. Her righteous wrath, my normal cowardice, and a spur from my conscience sent me out into the night, a poor match for the intrigues of Poe's imagination.

My throat was tight with terror by the time I had reached the garden gate. I decided to walk down the middle of the rough cobbled path that surrounded the village. If I kept too near the dry-stone garden walls, God knows what weird-faced apparitions might pop up over them. If I walked too near the ditched bank bordering the forest, I might be within arm's reach of the monsters and ogres hiding behind the trees.

I mustn't break into a run, even if my trembling legs could manage it; *that* would be acknowledging the retinue of evil spirits dogging my footsteps, waiting to pounce. Where, oh where was I going to get the courage not to run past the chapel?

There it was, half-way down the hill, a black sinister shape against the moonlit sky; just as on the cover of the book. Even the tree was there, a nearby oak, leafless and dying, its branches turned into creaking talons, from which hung the skeletons I knew would be visible when I got near enough.

It was such a long way to the next cottage gate, all of a hundred yards. Carry on, feet, one in front of the other; eyes, don't look to left or right – cows can see each side as well as in front – oh! I'm glad I'm not a cow. I've passed the chapel, I'm still safe, now if I can keep on to the bottom of the village, I shall hear the blessed sounds of men's voices in the pub, and see the light in Mr Meek's window, the first one up the main road, and my destination.

Mr Meek's family had grown up. He still worked in the pit, ran some sheep in the forest, and was a spare-time butcher, as well as doing a bit of local preaching. It needed a Christian spirit to be a butcher in our village; there couldn't have been much profit in it!

Now I was hoping he would be a very kind man, and let Mam have a shilling's worth of meat.

Fear must have lent me a pale and tragic air. Mrs Meek won him round to letting me have some bits of meat wrapped up in newspaper, in no time at all. I was sorry to step outside their warm little lamplit kitchen. Now I had again to run the gamut of terror.

I had the pleasure of knowing Mam would be relieved and pleased that I had got something for our Sunday dinner on tick. But I wished it had been a lump of cheese, or a bag of taters; anything but meat – meat was dead flesh – dead flesh came off corpses. The soft, newspaper-wrapped bundle felt obscene and revolting under my arm; just the bait to bring the evil spirits, witches, and ogres crowding back on to my trail. Why, tonight of all nights, was there not a singular, solitary soul about to keep me company? It was more terrifying than ever to pass the ghostly chapel again as I went up the hill. Better to risk the long arms of the forest ogres, than the ghost of Poe's skeleton, hanging from the dead tree, creaking eerily in a light night breeze.

Don't look right; don't look left; just look straight ahead, at the little square of diffused lamplight coming through the paper blind at Mrs Protheroe's window.

Walk in the rain-formed ditch near the bank; this was the furthest I dare get from the chapel without getting too near the trees. It was a night shelter for an old ewe, which got up in lumbering fashion and broke the quiet with its loud peeved baa-ing, and sent me sprawling into the ditch, parting me from the parcel of meat under my arm.

Perhaps I would have died of fright there, had Mrs Protheroe not come out of her cottage just then, with a lighted lantern, to make sure her fowls were shut in. The well-known, shadowy figure, and the little bobbing light were a beacon that gave me the whimpering courage to retrieve my parcel, the paper now broken in places so that I must touch the raw, dead flesh.

Quietly sobbing with relief, I found the strength in my rubbery legs to hurry up the hill whilst Mrs Protheroe was still about. She listened at my plaintive approach, and, holding up her lantern to see me by, enquired kindly: 'Be that you, Polly my wench – what's the matter?'

'I fell over a sheep; I didn't know what it was,' I sniffed. 'The meat's come all undone,' I added forlornly.

'Come on in a minute, and I'll see to it for you.'

Inside, in the sparsely furnished, spotlessly clean little living-room, a bright fire burned in a shining grate. By it sat Goggy, snow-white hankie in his misshapen hand, catching the fluid from his chronically watering eyes, as he read one of his favourite books by Jack London.

He turned the book over, to give me his kind attention. Mrs Protheroe rewrapped the meat in clean paper, and then asked Goggy if he would take the lantern, and escort me to our garden gate. She had sensed how scared I was. Without demur, Goggy got up from the fire, and we went. On his tender malformed feet, it was slow progress, but what did that matter? Goggy could talk of shoes and ships and sealing-wax, of cabbages and kings; and he asked me how I was getting on at school.

To this damsel in distress he was indeed a knight in shining armour.

'Good night, Poll,' he said kindly, holding the lantern at arm's length to light me part-way down the garden path.

'Good night, Gog, and thanks a lot,' I called back.

Only a few yards more of dark gardens, and I was indoors again; into the cosy lamplit room, with a fire that Mam had magically coaxed into a cheery blaze. 'I got a bit o' meat,' I said, proud to have redeemed myself a little.

I could tell Mam was mollified, though her tone was still a bit sharp, as she bade me sit on the corner of the steel fender and have a good warm. We'd all have to wait for our suppers as, thanks to me, the taters were still hard in the oven. However, she spread us all a piece of bread to be going on with.

Like a soldier home from the wars, I had no grumble. I was so happy to be back, safe and sound, in the tiny fortress ruled by Mam.

# Party's Over

In families like ours, there were only three important birthdays in your youth; the one marking your arrival into the world; the fifth, which meant you could go to school and leave a bit more room under mother's feet; and the fourteenth. This birthday meant, for a daughter, that she was old enough to get her feet under someone else's table; in the case of a son, that he could follow his father down the pit, thereby lessening a little the wrinkles in his mam's purse, but adding a few more to her brow from worrying about his safety. For girls, going into service was our only future. There was no employment for us in the village, and leaving home at fourteen was common to us all.

We didn't expect folk outside the family to be interested in birthdays. Top-form teachers, and especially ones like Miss Hale, were an exception. Every year, a batch of young faces above the wooden desks were replaced with new ones. Often the back of a departing child would bring an involuntary sigh, no doubt in some cases, a sigh of relief.

One playtime, a few days before my fourteenth birthday, Miss Hale kept me in the classroom. She wanted to know if I had one special chum. I had two, Gladys and Dolly. Gentle, even-tempered Gladys, with whom I never quarrelled, and Dolly, more my own sort, peppered with flaws, with whom I frequently fell out of friendship and back in again. I had just made up after a row with Dolly, so her name tripped out first on my tongue.

'Well, what I would like you to do,' said Miss Hale, 'is to ask your parents' permission if you can come home with me next Tuesday. It will mean getting back fairly late; but tell them I'll be in charge of you and see you get home all right. Tell your mothers to dress you up in your best bibs and tuckers.'

It was a mystifying request, but I would have done anything for Miss Hale. Every time I thought of it, I overflowed with pride and conceit, because she had let me paint brilliant scarlet poppies on some black satin cushion-covers for her home. She had brought the oil paints to school for me to do it in drawing-class. Miss Hale was a wonderful painter, and I knew she could have done the poppies much better herself. Besides, she gave me the remainder of the paints to take home for myself, *and* some brushes.

Father said that sort of paint was expensive. He sat down one evening, and had a go with me trying to paint a picture. His was so much better than mine, that I told him he should have painted the poppies for Miss Hale.

Mam was very impressed by the invitation, and determined by any means in her power that I should go tidy to school that day. She let me wear her treasured white silk blouse, given her by one of my aunties in service; and, if some of the rest of my plumes were borrowed, at least I went to school decked out in fine feathers on my fourteenth birthday. Dolly's mam had done much the same for her.

Our school had a small, railed, concrete play-yard for the infant classes. The rest of the school ran loose in break-times, to play on a dirt area hardened by pupils' boots; and on a small, natural greensward which reached to the forest's edge. But there was no hopscotch, leap-frog, skipping, or tag, for Dolly and me that day. Social butterflies must not get grubby.

When school was over, we stayed behind with Miss Hale, until an unfamiliar quiet enveloped the cluster of grey stone buildings. It was a two-mile walk to the house to which Miss Hale had recently moved. No doubt Dolly, as well as I, was hoping for the honour of carrying her case.

Neither of us got it. A car, a real *car*, with a man driving it, came up to the school gates. It was as big a surprise to us as the pumpkin coach was to Cinderella.

Showing no surprise, Miss Hale ushered us out of school, and into the two back seats. Dolly and I were too overwhelmed even to whisper our amazement. We just widened our eyes and nudged each other. The two miles were gone in no time. We stepped down from our seats with more than a touch of grandeur, then stood back politely while Miss Hale had a few words with the driver.

After our cottages, Miss Hale's house seemed of palatial size; it was of red brick, and looked nearly brand-new. Inside, all seemed very grand. We had a wash in a little sink with a tap and a small pink towel, so clean and pretty we wondered whether to use it or wipe our hands on the legs of our drawers. Unlike the bucket privies we were used to at home and at school, Miss Hale's house had a water lavatory with a chain to pull.

When we were ready, Miss Hale took us into the dining-room. Our eyes nearly popped out of our heads at the sight of the table. It was more like a picture than reality. Only a few spaces of white lace cloth showed between the pretty, flowered plates and sparkling glass dishes, filled with an assortment of tinned fruit, jelly, and blancmange. There was ham, brown *and* white bread-and-butter, a pink-iced cake, and even fancy iced biscuits. Our mouths watered, yet it seemed wrong to destroy, by eating, such a work of art as that tea-table.

'Come on, girls, pull yourselves up to the table; you must both be hungry by now.'

I had always regarded Miss Hale as a very special lady, but even I did not realise how near to the style of a queen she lived. She rang a little bell, and almost at once the maid came in with the tea. I knew the maid, although she was a few years older than I, and came from another village. Had I met her on a woodland path, I would have said ''ullo, Jean' to her, bold as brass. But here, in Miss Hale's house, and seeing her all dressed up in a black dress, with a little lace apron, I didn't have the nerve.

Of course, Miss Hale was quite friendly and easy-going with her, and told her to bring in a jug of boiling water to put in the teapot for a second cup. Mam had told me to be careful to mind my manners, which to me meant eating as little as possible, and that very daintily, but Miss Hale just kept putting stuff on our plates in a manner that showed we were expected to eat it up, and who disobeys a school-teacher?

Everything tasted so delectable there wasn't much of a problem with leftovers. In lieu of social polish, our appreciative appetites served as grace and thank you to our hostess.

In response to Miss Hale's bell, Jean came in, and cleared the table. Then Miss Hale fixed up what she told us was a ping-pong net across it. She gave us a little white ball, and a small round wooden bat each, and tried to show us how to play table-tennis. At first, much to our dismay, we sent the ball flying against the walls and ceiling. We were improving, and happily absorbed trying to master the skill needed for some nimble scoring, when Miss Hale told us the car was waiting to take us all to the pictures. The pictures! What a rich layer-cake sort of evening we were having!

But this evening, there was no walk through the woods. It was an occasion, a state arrival, in a motor car: stately seats, too, the dearest in the house, in the front of the balcony, at one-and-six a go.

The picture was called *Ben Hur*, one of the great silent classics.

The hero, Ramon Novarro, was unbelievably handsome. So, as far as our immature experience allowed, we ran, with him, the gamut of his sufferings and achievements. We wept for the cruelly treated galley-slaves in the great Roman Navy ships; we held our breath for the famous chariot race; we sat in awed reverence, as the hand of Christ passed over the face of the old harridan, transforming her back to innocent beauty. Billions of Hollywood dollars had been poured into this melting-pot of hokum, and Dolly and I made the most of the feast it provided.

When the show was over, and the lights came on, it was difficult to readjust; I did not feel myself at all. Miss Hale asked us if we had enjoyed ourselves. 'It was wonderful Miss,' we gulped, still husky from our weeping.

'Good night, miss, and thank you, miss,' we chorused when Miss Hale left us at her gate, while we were driven on to the village.

After exchanging good-nights with the driver, we walked up the rough track to our garden gate. Our stomachs were still happily digesting all the luscious food, and our minds were full of Ben Hur. Or, rather, mine, and, I suspected, Dolly's were full of Ramon Novarro. I had fallen in love with him, so it would be silly to find out if Dolly was laying claim to him as well. We both held our counsel; it was not the time or place to fight about whom he belonged to just then.

Accompanied as I was by the spirit of that brave, noble charioteer, I was sure there would be no witches or such-like hanging about behind the hedges or down the garden path tonight.

Mam and Dad were sitting by the fire, waiting to hear all about our visit to Miss Hale's. My tongue now ran on nineteen to the dozen about the wonders of the evening; the car rides, the lovely house, the food, the ping-pong game, the pictures.

'Well,' exclaimed Mam, 'all I can say is that Miss Hale's a thorough good 'oman to go to all that trouble and expense just for you, and because it's your birthday!'

Just for me! It had all been for my benefit! As I began to realise this was indeed so, it seemed the most wonderful surprise of it all.

On my very last day at school, I said goodbye to Miss Hale, and took a long look round at the familiar classroom, waiting until the school doors were locked behind me. All the rest of the children had gone when I walked slowly home through the Forest, a solitary mourner for my schooldays. The bony finger of poverty was pushing me out into an alien world, away from the little corner I knew and the family I loved.

Yet, since I had no choice about leaving, at least I was determined to be mistress of my own fate. I had heard about domestic service in Bristol or Cheltenham from older girls in the village. *I* was going to go to London.

A few weeks before my birthday, I'd answered an advertisement in the *Daily Herald* for 'a general maid fond of children'. I'd got the job, no doubt because of the very flattering testimonial supplied by Miss Hale. The address sounded very grand – a hundred and fourteen Mildmay Park Road, Stoke Newington. The people's name was Fox.

Mam was very concerned that I should be aware of my own status. 'You'll be a young 'oman,' she said, 'now you be goin' into service, and you'll 'ave to start bein' called by your proper name, Winifred. That's what you was baptised and registered by, not the paltry name of Polly your Dad give you.'

I did not want to be a young 'oman, a Winifred, I just wanted to stay a Polly. But I could not do that, so what did it matter what I was called? I promised Mam I would let my employers call me by my proper name.

Mam didn't get too alarmed about my going to London, as I had an auntie working in Westminster as a cook, and one of Dad's butties from the pit had told Mam in all seriousness that if I was to walk towards a place called Marble Arch, which was in the middle of London, on my half-day, I would be bound to bump into her; so she thought I wouldn't feel too lonely up there.

She did ask, very grumpily, where I thought the money was coming from to pay my fare all that way. As I was starting off at the big wage of six-and-eightpence a week, I wrote to Mrs Fox asking if she would forward my fare and deduct it at the rate of two shillings a week. I would still have four-and-eightpence left, and that was a lot of money to get used to all of a sudden. She sent back a pound by return.

In fact I was becoming a young person of means. For going-away presents I had a variety of things from several neighbours.

Two properly hemmed handkerchiefs, the first I had ever owned, that had sprigs of flowers in the corner. After a lifetime of using the inside of my skirt hem or sleeve, when no one was looking, it seemed sacrilegious to use these dainty, ironed white squares for wiping my nose. Then I had a comb with all the teeth in; a camisole, edged with lace, in good condition (I had nothing to fill it up with then, but the giver remarked that I would soon grow into it); and a much-battered tin trunk that looked very presentable when Dad had banged out the biggest dents with a hammer and Mam had worked herself into a sweat polishing it. Girls going into service had to provide their own black dress and white cap and apron, and this was a problem. Luckily Mam was able to make a swap. A young miner's wife, expecting her first baby, exchanged her maids' dresses for Mam's treasured washstand jug and basin set.

Wonderful as these gifts were, they didn't compare with what was in the brown paper parcel given me by Miss Hale – one of her coats, a hat, and a pair of shoes. Mam said they were as good as brand-new, and must have cost a mint of money.

So, a couple of weeks after my birthday, Mam rose at five-thirty to light the fire, that I might have a good warm, and some hot tea and toast, before we started our walk to the little station-halt a mile away. A good many ladies slumbering peacefully in their beds would have stirred uneasily in their sleep had they known what was on the way to try them.

Despite all my newly acquired material wealth, I'd never felt so poor in spirit. My little sister had woken when Mam called me, and now she sat on my lap, sipping my tea and nibbling little bits of my toast. To part from her warm little body seemed as terrible as parting with my head on a scaffold. I would have to wait a whole year before I could claim a holiday, and come home to my family again. A year was eternity!

The little room I sat in seemed the most desirable place on earth. I looked at the big black-leaded grate Mam took such pride in shining. In the oven door was set an emblem, a smiling face surrounded by rays – *smiling*, when I was going away! Sometimes Mam had made me clean the big steel fender and the fire irons with a damp rag dipped in the ashes from under the fire. 'Shine it till you can see your face in it' was her order, and a very sour, sullen face it reflected by the time I'd finished. Now I thought how lucky I would be to stay at home and rub a real sparkle into it. The dresser Dad had made stood there showing off the pride of Mam's household possessions: a teapot, jug and sugar basin got with labels saved from tea packets. The few wooden chairs, the well-scrubbed table, the rag hearthrug, old Auntie's two vases, showing angelic cherubs caressing beautiful Grecian ladies, standing at either end of the mantelpiece with the tea caddy in the centre, the religious texts, hung on nails around the walls, were no longer inanimate objects but *friends*.

Mam was much more chatty and friendly than usual and didn't

appear to notice that I only nodded my head to her remarks. My throat would choke up so. My young brother had woken early and come downstairs. 'I be comin' to 'elp you carry your trunk to the station,' he said.

'Well,' said Mam, 'we'll 'a' to be goin' soon or you'll miss your train. I'll pop in and ask Mrs Skinner to kip an eye on the two little'uns. You be gettin' your coat an' 'at on. One thing, you be startin' off nice and tidy. The people you be goin' to work for will think you've come from a nice respectable 'ome, wi' clothes like that on.'

Miss Hale's hat was a head-hugging cloche with rosettes of brown ribbon over the ears. It had sat nicely on her fluffy, thick golden hair, but on my plain brown basin-cut bob it came so far over my eyebrows that I had to lift it continually to see where I was going. The brown coat had fur collar and cuffs and one big fancy button at the waist. True, the cuffs came down to the tips of my fingers and the hem nearly to my ankles, and there was room, as the bus conductor says, for one more inside; but – 'Never mind,' said Mam, 'now you'll be gettin' your bellyful of good food, you'll soon be fillin' it, an' it'll last you for donkey's years.'

Mrs Skinner came in to fetch my little sister, and promised to keep an ear open for the baby, who was still abed. My flesh, where my sister had nestled against me, seemed to tear as Mrs Skinner took her.

'My, Polly, you do look a proper young 'oman in they clothes. If I didn't know 'twas you, I could pass you on the road wi'out recognisin' you.' This was not surprising, since very little of me was visible.

My tin trunk was a good deal heavier than its contents. Mam and my brother insisted on carrying it between them. I was dressed in style, and I must be sent off in style. I walked behind them and felt ashamed of my reluctance to go out into the world and get my keep and be a help to the family. Before he'd gone to work on the late shift, Dad had come upstairs to say goodbye. 'Be you still awake, old butty?'

'Yes, Dad.'

'Now I don't have to tell thee 'ow much your mam and I wish we could kip thee at 'ome. We don't worry about thee bein' a good wench; we know thee won'tst do anythin' to let thy old Mam and Dad down. Our worry is that the job might be no good. Now mind what I do say: if they do work thee too 'ard, or not give thee enough vittles, or be bad to thee in any way, thee drap us a line and we'll scrape the money up some'ow to get thee wum. O' course, thee'st got to remember thee doesn't know much about the sart o' 'ousework they people do want, so be willin' to learn and do thee best. 'Pon my soul, if thy old dad don't envy thee a-goin' to a place like London. Just thinka' the sights, an' the wonderful things they 'a' got up there. Mind thee'st kip thee eyes open, and remember it all to tell thee old dad about when thee'st come 'ome for thee 'olidays. A year do seem a long way at thy age, and it'll seem a long time to we at 'ome, but just you think o' the excitement when we all come to the station to meet thee.'

I had thought *this* journey to the station would be exciting too, all those weeks ago when the pound came from Mrs Fox for my fare, but as I walked behind Mam and my brother I could only think about Mam's shoes, and how they were downtrodden and worn out completely on one side. Her shapeless lisle stockings hung in loose folds round her thin ankles. Perhaps my new mistress would give me some left-off clothes to send home, as some of my aunties used to for Granny. I noticed, too, the thin knobbly legs of my brother, emerging like matchsticks from the legs of his patched trousers, and I remembered a time when he'd fainted and gone into a coma. Dad had run, like one gone mad, for the doctor. When the doctor came he said something about malnutrition, and I looked it up in the dictionary at school. Under-nourished, that's what it meant. Well, now I would be able to do something about it. Surely I could send home at least a shilling a week; that would pay for three extra loaves. Perhaps I could send more when I'd repaid the pound.

We passed the well and its bubbling spring, where I'd gone so often with a bucket; past the old slag heap, where poor crippled Absy David was killed by a fall as he scratched for tiny coals to keep his fire going; past the wood we called the Hain, where blackberries grew, the best always out of reach, but plenty left to blacken our tongues for weeks, and to scratch our legs to smarting, bloodstained soreness, and sometimes enough for a blackberry tart, when Mam could spare the sugar; past the old beech-tree in the bluebell wood – here, one rare and joyous Sunday, Mam had taken us for a picnic, a real picnic, lighting a fire, boiling eggs in a tin saucepan, and making a jug of tea with the water when the eggs were done.

On we went, up to the slope by Nelsons Green, and in a moment we should be able to see the station. Oh, if only some magic act had made it disappear! No, it was there. And so, miraculously, was Dad!

There he was, emerging from a side track on to our path. His face was grey with fatigue, and smudged with pit dirt embedded in the wrinkles, but his eyes shone with pleasure as I ran to him, delighted at the surprise. He was sweating, for he'd made a long and hurried detour.

'Bless my soul, I can't be a-kissin' thee wi' all that finery on. I'll spile it all wi' this pit dirt. But give I thee trunk. I don't think it'll matter if I puts 'un on my shoulder: Mam can dust'n off wi' 'er pinny on the station.'

Oh what a lucky girl I felt to be so loved! Full of pride, and misery, of good intentions, and fear of what was in store, full of overwhelming love for everyone and everything I was leaving behind, I stood bemused, watching the train chug to a halt. The little platform became the edge of the old world, the world I had known, as a child in the Forest.

# Part II

# In the East End

It seemed to me as though time itself paused a moment with that train. As it chugged away, the picture of the little group I was leaving behind etched itself through a blur of tears into my memory.

Although the plush upholstered seat in the train seemed most luxurious, I felt I had been sucked into an iron demon caterpillar, with a mad engine for a head, shrieking and puffing with indecent haste to take me away from home.

When we had gone past Gloucester station, all seemed lost. But I mustn't cry, oh, I *mustn't* cry, lest the woman sitting opposite should notice. She had not looked up from the book she was reading.

The train ate the miles up like a rapacious locust. Insatiable, it went on and on, in what seemed to be an everlasting journey. I was able to recognise that Swindon wasn't Paddington despite its size and bustle. After Reading I began to feel nervous. Surely, when I had been to London before, during the General Strike, it hadn't been quite so far as this? Perhaps the train had hurtled past London! I plucked up the courage to ask my travelling companion.

I think that lady might well be described as a retiring sort of person. She had retired into anonymity behind her book for the whole journey. I can't say a twinkle came in her eye exactly, but her mouth did crack open a bit like a smile when she assured me that we had not passed London, and would soon be at Paddington. I could tell she didn't come from my part of Gloucestershire by the way she spoke.

Mam had told me I was to mind not to move off the platform, or speak to a soul until Blodwen, whom my new mistress had arranged to meet me, introduced herself. Apart from what I had learned at school of the great and glamorous history of London, I had also gleaned from hearsay that it was full of thieves, pickpockets, and white-slave traffickers on the look-out for lonely girls. To be on the safe side I sat on my up-ended trunk on the platform, kept my hand in my pocket firmly clutching my handkerchief with the two-and-ninepence in it, and looked such a picture of misery I don't think I'd have stood a chance of being abducted if a slave-dealer had been about.

Soon all the other passengers had hurried purposefully off to their destinations.

'Campin' out for the night, then?' the engine-driver's mate called, as the train I had come on shunted out of the station.

'Where d'you come from, then?' asked a pimply-faced young porter, in a manner that showed he had no hopes of me as a potential tip. He didn't look anything to be afraid of, so I answered him, 'Gloucestershire.'

He looked me over with insolent deliberation. 'That's where the cheeses come from, ain't it?' He made it sound like an insult. 'Wot yer got in there,' he said, nodding at my trunk, 'a few swedes to gnaw at?'

I was spared any more of his baiting by the approach of a young woman who seemed to know immediately who I was. She must be Blodwen, who worked for a friend of my new mistress. Blodwen didn't look like my idea of a maid at all. Her good looks were hidden, rather than accentuated, by an overdose of lipstick, rouge, powder, and mascara. She had the first cropped hair I'd seen, and she wore a flapper-length black satin coat fastened with one big fancy button. She was in high-heeled black court shoes, and pink silk stockings. I was very impressed.

The porter wasn't. 'She come up to skivvy in the same place as you, then?' he asked her. Like me, he was ignorant of the fact that she really longed to be taken for an actress, and she was stung to the quick that he saw through her. So she advised him tartly, 'Mind your own bloody business! You clear off, and go and count your pimples!'

This, I realised, was a young woman of authority.

'You know it's Jews you've come to work for, don't you? Watch out they don't try to get most of your wages back selling you something. How much money have you got with you?'

I told her: two-and-ninepence. 'Jesus! is that all?'

I couldn't make her out. It was a lot of money, and when I thought how badly it was needed at home, I thought she had a cheek. Especially when she added, 'Lend me a shilling for our fares, gal. I'm broke. Don't tell your missus. She gave me our fares, but I spent some of it on stockings to meet you, mine had a ladder in 'em.'

I gave her a shilling; one-and-ninepence was plenty to last me a week. Then I'd really be in the money, even when the two-shilling deduction was made for the pound advanced for my train fare, I'd still have nearly five shillings left. Six and eightpence a week seemed like riches to me. I thought afterwards it wouldn't have been right for a self-styled actress to go about with a ladder in her stocking. She found my old tin trunk a handicap to her style, too, but somehow it had to be got to Stoke Newington.

The first bus conductor was not sympathetic. He wanted to know if we'd got lost from a safari expedition – his bus had no room for big game hunters' equipment. 'Good job we aren't. With you looking so much like a monkey we'd have shot you,' Blodwen spat at him.

The next conductor let us, and the trunk, on, but enquired sarcastically whose dead body it contained. 'A bad-mannered conductor's,' Blodwen informed him.

Much to my dismay, for the further we travelled into London the more hopelessly lost I felt, we had to get off that bus and get on another. The first conductor we approached let us put the trunk on his bus. He had a crony sitting near the door.

'D'you reckon,' he said, in a loud, mock-confidential whisper, 'that I've caught 'em red-handed with the loot? You've 'eard ain't you, about that break-in at the Tower? 'Alf the crown jewels stole, and *that*' – nodding to the trunk – 'is where they be 'idden.' This style of banter continued, with much apparently good-humoured repartee from Blodwen. But when we and the trunk were off the bus, and it was starting off again, she held out her hand with the coppers for the fare still in it.

'Bloody pair of smart alecs! We put one over on you,' she hollered after them.

Although much of my attention had been focused on Blodwen, marvelling at her self-possession, I had also been aware of the concrete jungle getting thicker round us. It seemed a mad place, where they had drowned the sky with the silhouettes of houses, houses so squashed together that they hadn't left room anywhere for a blade of grass, let alone a tree. Coming from a village where one door meant one dwelling (even if it were a one-up one-down cottage with a lean-to back-kitchen), I couldn't make out why Londoners wanted such huge places to live in. I mistook a block of flats for a single house. I'd never heard of people living in layers.

They had buried the earth under concrete, and instead of growing flowers for colour, the London women painted their faces. They were a clever lot – all of them – for how could they find their way about in such a maze? What a clever girl Blodwen is, I thought. I knew I should never be able to find my way out of London by myself.

'This is it – Mildmay Park Road,' announced Blodwen, as we turned into a road of tall, drab, narrow houses.

All I could think was it ought to be ashamed of itself, swanking with such a grand-sounding name. Misery Dark Road would have been a more appropriate name; it would at least have had the virtue of honesty.

'That's where I work,' said Blodwen, pointing to one of the houses. 'It's only three doors away from you, so I'll look out for you when you're shaking the mats in the back-yard. You look up to the top windows to see if I'm waving. You're having your half-day same as me, Wednesday. I go to the Shoreditch Olympia mostly; it's only sixpence for a seat in the gods, and the programme lasts three hours! It's Mary Philbin in *Drums of Love* next week.'

By now we had stopped, and Blodwen was knocking at the door. Never mind about the drums of love! My own heartbeats pounded in my eardrums – the moment had come, I had arrived at the threshold of my career.

For a moment a curtain was drawn back a little on a ground-floor window for an unfriendly, indifferent face to see who was knocking. Then another face looked out from a top-floor window.

'Here's your shiksa!' Blodwen called up. Then to me, 'Now mind, don't tell her I borrowed that shilling. See you Wednesday – I'm off now – these buggers always want you to do them a favour if you hang about.'

I had known Blodwen less than an hour, but it was terrible to see her walk away.

The door was opened by a woman whom I judged to be in her early thirties. She had very black hair, dark eyes, and sallow skin. She looked a bit foreign. I had wondered what Jews looked like; I had only heard of Shylock and the ones in the Bible. Meanwhile she summed up what was visible of me. The too-large coat and hat Miss Hale had given me got her first attention. 'Such a coat, and such a hat, on such a girl! How come?' said her expression, as though she price-tagged them by instinct.

Though I had thought the road was shabby, I was impressed by the width of the stairs, and its fancy-patterned oilcloth with no cracks or bare patches. At the top of the first flight of stairs she told me to put my trunk down on the landing. 'That's your room – that's ours,' pointing to the doors, 'and this is the lavatory.' She opened this door, and there I beheld a flush toilet with a chain, a roll of toilet paper on a holder fixed to the wall, and a warm little rug for your feet. Fancy that! A posh lavatory stuck up in the middle of a house! As we went on up, she showed me in the corner of the stairway a little sink with a tap over it. 'That's our water,' she said. I was duly impressed by these unheard-of conveniences, and I thought, well, I've got a job with people of quality after all! A rum lot, as well, I added when we got to the top of the house, and she showed me a very small kitchen, the living-room, and the parlour. My new mistress explained, 'It's better this way, then it's quieter for the woman in the bottom half of the house.' 'Fancy,' I thought, 'I've got an upside-down job in half a house!'

The master was out, but the two small children of the household were playing quietly in the living-room – a boy toddler, and a girl a couple of years older. They were beautiful, with dark curling hair and huge brown eyes. Even though they were plump and well dressed, they were a vivid reminder that I might never see my little sisters and brother again.

This time I couldn't stop the tears, but Mrs Fox, my new mistress, seemed to understand. She took me downstairs to my bedroom, and told me to have a little wash and then come upstairs for my supper.

I had heard too much about being in service from my aunties to expect much in the way of sleeping quarters. My room seemed a novelty just the same. It was the home of the family junk; travelling bags and hobby kits, dressmaking dummies and the spades and buckets of seaside holidays. In places the junk was stacked to the ceiling, but space was left for a little iron bedstead, and a small, marble-topped washstand. There was a row of hooks behind the door for hanging clothes.

Mrs Fox had told me to put on my black afternoon dress and white apron. I kept trying to staunch the tears with the flannel and water in the washstand bowl. A black frock seemed to suit the occasion. I was in mourning for my lost self. I was in a strange new world – in a different role – with entirely new people to adjust to. My childhood was dead – now I was the skivvy – I was near to wishing she were dead too.

I was given my supper in the tiny kitchen while the family ate in the living-room. It was strange to be considered not fit to eat in the same room as other human beings. It was a good supper, a thick soup with butter beans in it, but loneliness and misery had taken away my appetite. How delicious, in comparison, seemed the remembered slice of marge-spread toast given me by Mam and eaten as a member of a family.

I was glad when I was told to go to bed; now I could squash my face into the pillow to smother the day's pent-up tears. Dr Johnson may have found in London 'all that life can afford', but all I could think was, 'what a bloody 'ole to come to.'

Having from time to time worked for Jewish people, I have a soft spot for them. It has been my experience, however, that they do like to think they have a bargain. Poor Mrs Fox, with six-and-eight a week to pay in wages, plus my keep, certainly had no bargain in me.

As far as domestic skills were concerned she had drawn a blank. Her standards of spit-and-polish were very high, and she lost a fair bit of fat showing me, by example, how to do each chore. On the first morning, I don't think she had the breath left to tackle the stairs, so she sent me to a special cut-price Jewish shop for some eggs.

Through the kitchen window overlooking the street she pointed out the direction. From there it seemed simple enough – second turning on the right past the chemist's, then first on the left till I came to Bloom's stores. I felt very proud of my achievement when I found the shop.

Bloom's stores seemed to contain things from all over the world, packed higgledy-piggledy into a long, dark-brown interior. There was only a very narrow space in front of a counter piled with goods for the customers, four of whom were already lined up inside. Pickled herring, paraffin, candles, cakes, matzo meal, washing-soda, pulses, spices, fats, flours, foreign-sounding food dried, tinned or packed, and eggs at fourteen for a shilling! The smells were indescribable confusion, once inhaled never forgotten!

A little old woman, almost indistinguishable from the surrounding brownness, hindered rather than helped by a similarly brown little old man, had got themselves in a right tangle. They searched their haphazard stock for some item for the first customer.

Despite the spectacles perched on the end of his long nose, the old man kept knocking things over in his futile effort to find what the customer wanted. With supplicating outstretched hands, the old woman begged the rest of us not to go away.

I was in no hurry – I found the whole spectacle very funny, and became most interested in the success or failure of the search. But I never found out the result.

Eventually the old man pushed by to ask what I wanted. 'Seven eggs for sixpence,' I told him. He seemed so disappointed he couldn't sell me anything else it was just as well my mistress had only given me the bare sixpence! The trouble was, he gesticulated his disappointment so strongly, he knocked an egg off the top of the box on to the floor and it broke.

I think those eggs must have come a long way, and taken their time about it; probably across the sea. Their insides were so pale, with a slight suggestion of green, that it was difficult to tell the yolk from the white. It must have been one from this shop Mrs Fox had given me for my breakfast. As I ate alone, I was able to pop down to the lavatory with my mouth full and pull the chain on the contents. I wasn't fussy about food, but those eggs took some swallowing.

As soon as I stepped on to the pavement from Bloom's stores, I knew I was lost. I couldn't remember from which direction I had come, and to my uninitiated eye, all the houses looked the same. I hurried a few yards in one direction, panicked, then tried the other way. I asked an old lady the way to Mildmay Park Road but she just ignored me. I did think of going back to ask the shopkeepers, but they seemed to have enough troubles of their own when I'd left them.

I had been used to taking my bearings by the different characteristics of familiar trees, banks, grasses, mosses and ferns; each woodland path was so different. Streets were all the same. Even when I summoned up the courage to ask other passers-by for directions, it was more by luck than by understanding that I got back into Mildmay Park Road just as an irate Mrs Fox was coming to look for me.

I proved what a duffer I could be when I had been there about three days. The family were going out for the afternoon and evening, and I should be on my own. To make sure I wasn't idle, Mrs Fox gave me a list of jobs to do. Before they went, she herself boiled up a bucket of soda-water on the gas stove. I was to take that stove to pieces, all of it, the top, and the oven, and thoroughly scrub all the parts in this soda-water; then wash out the kitchen and a flight of stairs. After that I could go in the living-room and clean the silver and brasses.

Gas stoves, in those days, were made entirely of black iron. I was completely ignorant about gas except to know that it was an explosive element, and that the jets made a little pop as they were turned off. I was scared stiff of them. However, I did as I was told and took the stove to pieces in my fashion, thoroughly scrubbing each piece in the soda-water, then piling them up on a wad of newspapers put ready on the little kitchen table. It was quite a pile-up by the time I'd done the last piece, and a thick topping of grease floated on the bucket of water, now barely lukewarm. What the gas company had put together, I had pulled asunder.

I was soon in a sweat, more from apprehension than from my labours, as I tried to fit the thing back together. I was very scared that if I put the wrong piece in the wrong hole I might blow the kitchen up. I decided to leave the bad alone, and scrub the floor and stairs down. It would have to be in fresh cold water as I couldn't heat any up. First I must empty the bucket, so I tipped the greasy water down the little sink in the corner. At least, that was my intention, but the sink only gave me its half-hearted co-operation. Some of the water disappeared, but the rest stopped, dark and greasy to the rim of the sink.

'Oh, my Gawd,' I panicked, 'what've I done now?' I'd ruined the sink as well as the gas stove! It was the first sink I'd ever had any dealings with; how could I know they suffered from constipation? Suddenly I remembered the hymn we had been taught in our teetotaller's meetings:

Pull for the shore, sailor, pull for the shore
Heed not the rolling waves, but bend to the oar

I bent to wash the floor and stairs with my bucket of cold, grease-speckled water; trying to rally out of my despair with a quaking rendering of that hymn. My tears splashed into the bucket. Too daft to think of pouring this bucket of water down the lavatory, I left it to decorate the landing.

I had one straw of hope left – I would clean that silver and brass as it had never been cleaned before, in an effort to make amends. It was getting dusk, and I should need to see what I was doing. I had seen Mrs Fox put a light to the gas-mantle, so, taking a match, I followed suit. I struck the match and pushed it into the mantle, which instantly disintegrated, as daintily as snowflake powder, on to the mat.

Now, I *had* done it! Equating fragility with expense, I thought I must have bankrupted my wages for months. Only, how would I have any wages? I'd get the sack; nobody could be expected to put up with such a booby. What would I do? I'd no money to get home, even if I'd known how to get there.

Then I thought of Blodwen. I'd only seen her once, when I was mat-shaking in the back-yard, and her face in the window had been as welcome as sunshine after rain. Desperation made me think – I would go and knock on the door of the house where she worked, and throw myself on Blodwen's mercy. I ran down the stairs, and left the front door ajar. With a heart pounding at my own boldness, I knocked on the door of number 108. All the windows were in darkness. I knocked again, and again, and again. It was no good – they must all be out. I got back just as a draught caught the front door and it banged shut in my face.

I was now locked out. Perhaps it was as well, really. At least I couldn't do any more damage out here! I didn't feel I had any right to be stuck on the pavement either, though I stepped apologetically out of the way of passers-by. They took no notice, of course. It was as difficult to be conspicuous in London then as it is now. The time passed in a kind of black limbo, between the sins I had committed indoors, and the retribution to come.

I must have had water on the brain; I started to cry again as soon as the Foxes walked up towards me. To my incredible surprise and relief, Mrs Fox seemed more annoyed at my miserable reaction than she did about my misdeeds. If she had not been my mistress I would have loved to hug her in gratitude. She put the stove back together in no time, and pooh-poohed the idea that a gas-mantle was a precious object. Then she got me to ladle the greasy water out of the sink, and put a packet of soda into it. She boiled up a kettle on the reconstituted stove, and poured it over the soda. After some gurglings and belchings the sink relieved itself, and me.

In a back-handed way, that calamitous afternoon did me a good turn. I still had the silver to clean, and I was allowed to stay in the living-room with the family while I did it. The children watched me, and in no time I was making them laugh with silly rhymes, and drawing things in their crayon books. The silver took a long time; but, after that, I was allowed in with the family to keep the children company. Soon the Foxes were able to go out for an evening, knowing I would keep the children happy and safe.

The next day was Wednesday, my half-day. As though she hadn't been kind enough, Mrs Fox gave me the four-and-eightpence wages due a day in advance. I still had my one-and-ninepence, and I decided to ask Blodwen to take me to a post office so I could put a three-shilling postal order in my letter home. Those three shillings seemed like a silver lining showing through at last.

I was ready to go down when Blodwen knocked at the door. She was made up to the nines again, and wearing a new pink silk blouse. 'Come on, gal, step it out. I want to get meself a new hat to match this blouse, before we go to the pictures.'

I don't suppose it's practised now; but in those days, if you passed outside a shop in the East End to look at the window display, you were literally pulled inside, and cajoled, beseeched, and nearly threatened, to buy something. Resistance was difficult, but Blodwen managed it. 'Get off,' she threatened, 'or I'll put my bloody shoe through your window.' Eventually, after much window-shopping, and peering into the interiors, Blodwen decided on a shop to get her hat. It was a small shop, run, apparently, by one assistant.

Hundreds of hats were piled in a long trough-like counter, for the customers to pick and choose. The fashion then was for head-hugging felt hats in the style of a Roman soldier's helmet. There were several colours, and various trimmings.

The prodigal son couldn't have got a more effusive welcome than we did from that shop assistant. It seemed that her shop had the very hats that could have been exclusively designed for two such young ladies.

Had I been buying a hat, I would have suited myself in a matter of moments. But not Blodwen. She tried on hat after hat for so long that I began to feel quite sorry for the assistant. Not one of them was exactly what Blodwen wanted. Could she try that pink one in the far corner of the window? The one so difficult to get at?

Desperately determined to make a sale, the poor woman wriggled herself through the window display to reach it. My stomach couldn't stand any more of Blodwen's brand of sadism. 'I'll wait outside for you,' I told her.

She came out of the hat shop just in time to catch me being frogmarched into the next-door gowns and mantles emporium by two saleswomen; despite my entreaties that I had no money to spend.

Blodwen got hold of me by the back of my coat collar and yanked me away. 'You can be had up for kidnapping you know,' she threatened the two women. 'Come on, let's get a move on, the bloody picture'll have started.' She hustled me down the street.

'Did you buy that hat out of the window?' I asked.

'Who said anything about buying a hat?'

My puzzled response to this remark got me an impatient shove. 'Wait till we get out of sight of here, then I'll show you.' And show me she did. Two hats, one pink (but not the one from the window) and one brown were in her shopping bag. 'This one's for you,' she said, handing me the brown one.

'D'you mean to say you stole them?' I asked incredulously.

''Course I did,' she laughed, 'that's why I got the silly old bloodsucker to get that one out of the window, so's I could pop these in my bag. Ten-and-six she wanted for that pink hat in the window – bloody cheek – she must have seen me coming! Daylight robbers, that's what they are.'

I put the hat back in her bag as though it were a live viper. Oh dear, whatever would my Mam and Dad have said if they could see me now going out with a thief, and a Welsh one at that? Mam was very proud of being Welsh, and depicted them all as a cut above anybody you could find in Gloucestershire. When she had a bit of a shindig with Dad, didn't she always taunt him that 'she indeed had come from a respectable family'. I'd never be able to tell Mam about Blodwen.

We didn't have a policeman in our village but in a place the size of London they probably had a couple of dozen. Any minute I half-expected the hands of a pair of them to come down heavily on our shoulders.

I was glad when we came to the picture house; the police'd never find us in that great place.

It wasn't exactly the gods; it was steps that served for both purposes. Peanut shells and sweet wrappings crackled under our feet, as Blodwen found us a space to sit. The tang of orange peel fought with tobacco and the warm body odour rising from the stalls and balcony.

Between the films there were live turns, and these had just started. I was bewitched with surprise and delight; soon stolen hats, my domestic shortcomings, and even homesickness faded from my consciousness.

There was a troupe of Japanese jugglers, made exquisitely miniature and deft by the distance. Next came three trim girl dancers, tapping out their lively dances with identical precision. I was spellbound.

Anna Rogers, the fifteen-year-old wonder girl, came next. She seemed uncannily clever. She must have been. She was only sixteen when I saw her name on a playbill in South London five years later.

'Not bad turns this week,' observed the sophisticated Blodwen. '*Not bad!*' They were magic people, so clever, so beautiful! Aladdin himself couldn't have been more dazzled, when the Genie's lamp transported him to the treasure cave, than I was that first night in the Olympia picture house, Shoreditch.

The film, *Drums of Love*, was completely lost on me. The heroine lying about on skin-covered divans, languishing for whatever it was she was missing, didn't have my sympathy.

Before she emerged into the spotlight of public gaze, Blodwen had to make up her face again. How drab and insignificant everything seemed, compared with the world of stage and screen!

The ladies' cloakroom smelled dusty, and stale with cheap perfume. 'Can I wait outside, on the steps?' I asked Blodwen, as she daubed on the Phul-Nana. She nodded absently, then tried to add yet more mascara to her eyelashes.

I stood alone on the steps that led up to the paybox. I was storing into my memory the wonder of those stage turns, so that I might tell Dad and Mam, if I ever got home again. My musings were interrupted by two young lads, apparently in a state of agitation.

'Eh, miss! Our friend's fainted down that alley. Will you come and see if you can 'elp him?'

'Oh dear, poor boy,' I thought. I had seen children faint in school and be carried to lie down by the stove near teacher's desk. Teacher would roll up her coat and make a pillow, and sponge the child's face with cold water.

So, I had started down the steps with them, when Blodwen came out and demanded where the hell was I going? The boys melted into thin air.

Anxious to help, I was all for taking Blodwen down the alley to find the fainting boy.

'Jesus! It's me that's going to faint, being landed with a turnip-head like you! Honest, gal, you're greener than my Mam's cabbage after she puts the soda in. *Don't* you *ever* go anywhere with anybody, especially boys that you don't know.'

If Blodwen found me a puzzle, I found her peculiar notions were puzzling, too. What harm could possibly have come to me going down a back-alley to help a boy who'd fainted? From my gentle father, and the kindly men of our mining village, I had learned nothing to make me beware a man's advances.

But I didn't argue with Blodwen. I was so glad of her company, and so grateful for it, that I felt it only fair to do as she told me. Except for taking a stolen hat; I had to draw the line somewhere.


Despite the weekly excitement of my half-day, and the fact that sometimes I had to go over my chores only twice to pass muster, I was terribly homesick. I had been used to playing with, picking up, and generally loving, two little sisters and a brother; and receiving affection from them, from my parents, and from my playmates. Much as I liked the two children of my master and mistress, I was sensitive enough to realise that I could not show them the warmth that I could express at home.

After many weeks, when I could find an odd corner to myself, I still let the tears run. I knew exactly what the expression 'a heavy heart' meant. Mam wrote to me every couple of weeks. These letters were my lifeline; pieces of paper to treasure, to keep alive the hope that one day I would get back home.

That day came. When I had been with Mrs Fox for about three months, I had a letter from Mam saying my four-year-old sister was ill again with pleurisy.

I was learning to live with homesickness, but I could not contain this additional blow. When my little sister was two she had been for a spell in a sanatorium, and had become brown, plump, a picture of health. But each winter since, she had had this terrible illness. How could she get better, if I weren't there to help run upstairs with the hot linseed-meal poultices for Mam to put on her as fast as Dad could make them?

I was so distraught that I could not speak coherently when Mrs Fox asked me what was the matter. She took the letter and read it. My grief went to her kind heart. 'You shall go home,' she said. 'Pack your clothes, and I'll get Blodwen to take you to the station. Have you got your train fare?' I shook my head; I had not saved up enough in the time. 'Never mind,' she said, 'I'll make it up. When your little sister is better, promise you'll come back and work for me.'

In view of my deficiencies, her request was one small proof of the Jewish ability to stand suffering. I promised her that I would. I would have promised anyone anything without a scruple, as long as I could get home to my little sister. But I had no intention of coming back.

Kind Mrs Fox! She made up a parcel of warm vests and clothes from her children's plentiful store. I took all her kindness; and I'm ashamed to admit I never even wrote to her.

Blodwen said she would miss me, and insisted on me taking the brown hat home. She told me of all the people she had known in Wales who had got over pleurisy. She got me, quivering with fear lest I miss the train, into Paddington with time to spare.

I told her she was better, and more like an actress, than Mary Pickford. I felt so grateful to Blodwen, and all I had to give her was a compliment.

The train, which had seemed so mad to take me away from home, did not go half fast enough as it huffed and puffed its way westward.

# An Old Lady

When I reached Cinderford, and began the walk home, I realised how much I had seen, how many new sights and sensations I had absorbed in those few months in London.

I had seen a mountain to measure a molehill by. The little shop, whose window had contained a lifetime's indulgences of sweet-tooth delights, where the decision how best to spend a penny had kept me drooling with anticipation for a quarter of an hour, was now just a pokey little sweet shop.

The endless greensward to the old brickworks was but a quarter-mile's walk of rough open sheep-grazing pastureland. The single-line railway track that cut across it, with Wimsey Halt station shelter for waiting passengers, was as small and poor as a child's plaything. Everything seemed to have shrunk in that forest clearing; all the better for my hurrying feet to get me home and to my little sister's bedside.

The old magic came back as I entered the last part of my walk, through the forest surrounding our village. There they stood, the oaks, unchanged and beautiful, living statues of nature's architecture. Even Sir Christopher Wren could fashion nothing to match them.

*Now* I was back home. But oh, how pitiful, how small, home seemed! How little and worried Mam looked, as she took me straight upstairs to my sister. ''Er've 'ad the crisis; 'er's on the mend, thank God, so doosn't worry now,' Mam comforted me.

Sweat-dampened strands of dark hair clung to the forehead of the little, wizened, wasted face in the bed, bereft of the plump contours of healthy childhood, all mouth, and great, sad, heavy eyes.

I, great, blubbering, homesick coward, had come back home, penniless and jobless, to lessen still further the chances of comfort for those I professed to love. As I sat on the bed and hugged her, I made a resolve. I would get a job at once. If it was the worst place in the world, I'd stick it for at least six months. I wrote right away for another job; this time, in the Cotswolds.

Prepared now for the heartache of home-sickness after my first short-lived job, but determined to stay in this one for six months whatever the conditions, I put down one hundred and eighty-three lines on a piece of paper – every night I could look forward to crossing one off.

Now one hundred per cent willing, if not very able, I started my job as general maid to an old lady in the Cotswolds. I was fourteen years old and just emerging from my first childhood – she was ninety-one and tottering into her second, so we got on pretty well together. Her treatment of the long string of unfortunate girls who had preceded me had given her a local reputation for being a 'cantankerous old tartar'.

Actually age had softened the old tyrant quite a bit. I was the first maid allowed to sleep in one of the bedrooms. The others had had to make do on an old palliasse on the floor of the attic. I found this out when she poked me awake with her walking-stick in the small hours to tell me there was a burglar up there.

If there was I didn't intend to disturb him.

With lighted candle in hand I climbed up through the trap door. I banged about a bit to give the illusion of inspection, clambered down and firmly announced, 'Not a sign o' a skerrit of any sorts up there ma'am.'

Because of her rheumatics I had to act as 'kneel in' for the old lady's prayers. I thought she had a fat chance of getting to heaven with that attic on her conscience and two spare bedrooms in the house! But she was old and pitiful, so just in case there was a God up there listening I put in a plea for her on the quiet.

She was a proper old termagant for waking me up in the night on one pretext or another. Eventually she asked me to sleep with her in her big four-poster bed.

I had to undress her at night. It was a long business – nature's whittling had left very little under the voluminous layers of clothes. Her false teeth came out first – then her false hair which was attached to a goffered white headpiece in the manner of Queen Victoria. After I had removed the layers of day clothes and helped her on to the night commode, I had all the rigmarole of dressing her up for the night. Woollen vest, flannel chemise, nightgown, bed jacket and bedsocks; lastly a white silk scarf over her poor little balding head tied under her chin in case she died in the night – she didn't want the indignity of being found with her mouth agape. After that it was gently heaving her up into the great four-poster bed.

Before I could get in, I had to go through the nightly ritual of making sure every door downstairs, even the one at the bottom of the stairs, was chained and padlocked. As the windows were lead latticed, I kept assuring her that Tom Thumb couldn't get in, let alone a burglar. It was a bit disheartening after all that trouble to be poked awake a couple of hours later to do a bit of exorcising. She used to wake up saying she was having horrible visions and the only way I could get rid of them was for me to walk slowly round the bed three times saying prayers.

She had a great dread of dying and confessed this to me one day.

'Don't you fret about that ma'am,' I comforted her, lying like a trooper on the spur of the moment, 'my old Great-Auntie come to me in a vision and told me'twas like goin' to sleep in a coal'ole and wakin' up in a palace.' The times I had to tell her that fib, adding bits I 'remembered', to convince and further reassure her.

At first I ate my food in the kitchen, but she had to ring her bell so often for me to mop up the mess she made, that soon she sacrificed dignity for expediency and said I could eat in the dining-room with her. 'Don't go getting big ideas that you are a lady's equal,' she warned me. Such a remote possibility had never entered my head!

My old mistress had to live on a very small pittance allowed her by her nephew in London. She was childless, and had been a widow for many years. Her sea-captain husband had left his money invested in German railway stock. It had gone up in smoke in the First World War.

Every year the nephew came down to make sure she had not altered the will leaving the cottage and its contents to him. Her longevity was obviously getting on his nerves, but he was still getting a bargain.

The cottage was a gem of Cotswold stone with lattice windows set in a quarter of an acre of walled garden. The kitchen was separated from the dining-room by the parlour. The access door from the kitchen to this middle room was kept locked, so I had to run across the yard with the food. In a downpour the gravy got watered down a bit.

The garden bloomed with the glory of an English cottage garden. It seemed to contain a little of everything: winter jasmine to autumn chrysanthemums – with crocuses, daffodils, narcissi, lily-of-the-valley, primulas, pansies, snapdragons, canterbury bells, sweet-williams, carnations, pinks, mignonette and lavender, some cultivated, and some which had sown themselves of their own sweet will in unexpected places. Also there were a green and a rosy apple tree; red-, white- and black-currant bushes; white and dark pink raspberries; three sorts of gooseberries and four rows of strawberries.

In the spring the rows of young vegetables were like fancy stitching on the earth's dark petticoat – rosettes of baby lettuce; the feathery stitch of young carrot tops; spiky stitch of spring onions, and the dainty embroidery of red-edged baby beetroot leaves. An old man came two days a week for a shilling a day to keep it all in order. He made up for his small wage by nicking a lot of the produce. Very conscious of the capitalist structure of our society, I turned a blind eye to this until I felt he was overstepping the mark, and robbing my old mistress who was also poor. I ticked him off. Fifty-fifty from then on, or I threatened to spill the beans.

Though the old lady ate very little herself it was still a struggle for her to pay my one pound a month wages. 'Don't you fret ma'am, a plate o' taters wi' a knob o' marg would suit me fine for dinner,' I often told her.

In those days the baker's man called every day. Twice a week she took a fresh batch loaf from him, sometimes still warm from the oven. To sit with her in that dining-room with the sun streaming through the lattice window, watching the japonica blossoms nod against the panes, eating crusty buttered newly-baked bread, and drinking tea made with fresh spring water from a silver teapot, feasting the eye on a standard tea-rose through the open door, made up for a lot of my life's drawbacks.

There were other pleasures too. I never had any time off, but once a month she sent me into Stroud to get a freshly laundered headpiece from a little widow woman who did the hand laundry. At the same time I could send a postal order home to Mam and buy myself black stockings or a pair of shoes. To save her the tuppence fare I offered to walk – and so had three miles each way that was sheer delight from start to finish.

A white rose growing over the remains of a tumble-down cottage had gone into ecstasies free from the pruner's knife. In late spring, wall-flowers, tawny velvet to brilliant flame, burst from crevices in dry-stone garden walls. Sometimes a lady in one of the gardens would bid me a pleasant 'good afternoon'. Of course, they didn't know I was a mere skivvy. It was nice to be spoken to as an ordinary human being.

As well as the wonders before my eyes, I had all the wonders of a dream future to ponder on. I never stinted myself in this field. A dawdler by nature, I didn't have to worry about stepping it out, as a neighbour from a nearby cottage got my mistress tea on these occasions. This same woman had 'obliged' when there was a gap between the arrival of a new maid and the departure of the last one. All the same I mostly got a tart scolding for my lateness.

In my early days there, on Sunday mornings, I had to help my mistress up the hill to the nearby church, leave her at the door and be there to collect her when the service was over. Later on she sent me in her stead, sitting in for her in her pew, six rows from the front. There was too much to be done for me to attend morning service. I went in the evenings instead.

Regurgitated through the rector's monotonous sing-song, I found the words of the Bible illogical and meaningless. 'Blessed are the meek for they shall inherit the earth.' I wondered when? The snobby lot sitting in the front few rows looked as though they had got a good whack of it, and there was nothing meek about *them*. I found no comfort for my spirit in the service, but I found an object for my romantic notions on the organ stool. He was young, incredibly handsome, with a profile like Ivor Novello's and so remotely inaccessible that he was just right for my daydreams.

I evolved a wonderful daydream around that young organist. I sat in a lovely cottage on top of a hill with a cliff-face going down to the sea. In a delightfully cosy room with frilled muslin curtains, a glowing fire, a table laid with the daintiest of teas on a snowy-lace cloth, and a baby like a living doll in a cradle by the side of the hearth, I waited for the young organist – now transformed to a bronzed young sea captain. Smart as paint in his uniform, he was hurrying up the cliff-face to the baby, home and me. Never a thought as to how this situation came about, or how my daydream would continue, intruded upon my mind.

Next to crossing a tick off my piece of paper every evening, I looked forward to going to church. Until one evening, perhaps by some kind of telepathy, the young man turned his head and seemed to look straight into my eyes. It was a cool, patronising stare, as though he'd sensed the boldness of my thoughts. I felt terrible, like a criminal caught in the act. I nearly keeled over in the pew with faintness.

After that, I persuaded my mistress to let me give her a proxy sermon at home. She didn't really like being left alone, so she agreed. Because she couldn't kneel down, I had to kneel on a higher chair than the one she sat on, to give the illusion of a pulpit. Imitating the intoning manner of the rector, I crucified the words even better than he did, but she was well satisfied.

I love the courage of old age, illogically struggling on with the daily grinds of living when they're no longer important. What mattered a few cobwebs to my old mistress? Yet she told me that the cottage must be spring-cleaned, starting with the dining-room. I had never heard of spring-cleaning, but I soon knew all about it, and how!

First the polish had to be made. Under her supervision, I boiled up a mixture of beeswax, vinegar, and linseed oil. Polish is a misnomer for this product, it's the elbow grease necessary to rub off its dulling patina where the shine comes in.

The dining-room was not large, but it was very crowded. Apart from ornaments, pictures, and knick-knacks, there were a good many items of furniture. One wall was almost taken up with a magnificent Chippendale bookcase, usually kept locked.

Now I had to take every volume outside, open it, bang it shut in case it had gathered dust, then rub the leather covers. It was a lengthy business; every time I went outside, the fresh beauties of the garden, the view of the gently undulating hills and valleys, and the warmth of the sun, made me slower than ever.

The dining-table had been made from a huge slice of mahogany, and had no join. If that table is now in the possession of some lucky owner, they can thank me for helping with its preservation. Drops of my sweat went into the polishing of it. I have swept enough dust under the carpet in my time to fill a few window boxes, and concentrated my energies only on the parts of objects that showed – but there was no dodging this job! It was too big to take outside, and under the old lady's strict eye, perfection was the target.

The old man who did the gardening helped me to hang the faded carpet over the clothes line. She sat on a chair by the door to make sure I whacked the hell out of it. Then it was laid on the flagstoned yard, and sprinkled with a thick layer of salt and used tea-leaves, saved for the purpose. It was left like that while we had our dinner. Then I had to brush off every tea-leaf with a small hard brush, and go over it with a cloth wrung out in a bucket of water laced with vinegar to restore the faded colours, then hang it on to the line to dry.

I had to scrub the tiled floor underneath three times with hot soda-water before I was allowed to polish the surrounds till the sunlight brought a sparkle to the tiles.

Every job took ages. I had all the time in the world. My mistress was irritable because hers was running so short. She would ring her handbell angrily, and threatened me with her walking-stick for my dallying. 'Ketch me first,' I thought.

She did one day. I'd found a copy of *Uncle Tom's Cabin* in the attic during one of my burglar-hunting excursions. She never gave me a minute's peace to read, so I hid it on a shelf in the kitchen cupboard. All my chores in there were done slapdash quick, so that I could have a read. The tap-tap of her stick across the yard warned me of her approach.

One day I got so engrossed in the part where Eliza braves the frozen river with her little son in her arms that I was indeed deaf to the world around me, the scalding tears falling on a pile of plates already inadequately wiped. I came smartly back to earth with a stinging swish from her walking-stick across my behind. She'd had a lot of practice, so was quite a markswoman despite her age. My uncontrollable fit of crying against the cupboard door, for I'd not yet found out if Eliza got safely across, took my old mistress by surprise. She was quite contrite. I didn't bother to enlighten her – she might find me with my head stuck in the cupboard again!

In those days, maids were two-a-penny, yet enticing a maid away was common practice. On one occasion, the old lady's nephew, his wife, and his two daughters came to stay for a week.

The day before they left to go back to London, the nephew's wife came into the kitchen, all smarm and charm, to tell me I'd be much happier in London working for them. She gave me a stamped envelope addressed to her, for me to let her know when I'd be coming. I was not to tell the old lady.

When she went out, I stared into the little mirror in the kitchen to see if I looked as big a simpleton as she took me for.

Another relative tried it on too. She was quite a charming maiden lady, who had been left very well off and lived in a small select house somewhere in Sussex. I can't think why, but she reckoned I was just the sort of girl she'd been looking for. If I went to her, I would be more than a maid, a sort of lady's companion. She had a local woman to do the rough work. She also hinted that if I stopped with her, it would eventually be much to my material advantage.

Even the rector had a dab at it.

I was picking runner beans for dinner one day, when he came up the garden path after a visit. He stood there, humming and hawing about the weather and God's bounties of the earth, but he soon got onto his own tribulations. The housemaid was leaving the rectory; if I wanted a better job, it was mine.

I haven't much time for the clergy on the whole, especially those who get up on a Sunday morning to cleaned rooms, lit fires and a good big breakfast cooked for them by the meek in heart in the back regions of the house.

'No thank you,' I told him.

All this again was said behind my old mistress's back, which killed the notion from the start, as far as I was concerned.

Though I had some loyalty to my mistress, some pity, if not quite affection for her, it didn't stop me giving her my month's notice when the six months was up. I should have to wait another six months before I had earned the annual two weeks holiday she allowed. But I knew I couldn't bear the separation from my family that long.

She autocratically pooh-poohed the idea. I told her I meant it, and she must start looking for another maid. She did nothing of the sort. She gave me a sort of bribe, a fine wooden needlework casket, with a sampler in it, which she had worked at the age of six. I felt I could not accept it and gave her my notice in writing. I had heard my aunties say this made it legal. She threw it on the fire. Two more weeks of longing to get home went by, and it was my afternoon to walk into Stroud. I was upstairs getting ready when I heard footsteps on the yard, and got the surprise of my life to see my elder sister, Bess, standing there.

'Where be the old varmint?' she asked.

I nodded towards the dining-room door.

'I be come to fetch thee wum.'

'I can't come,' I wailed, 'she's got nobody yet to take my place.'

'Nor likely to, you sawney hap'orth, as long as you be muggins enough to stop 'ere. Where's your things?'

'Up here,' I told her, 'but my box is in through the kitchen there.'

'Chuck thee things out through the winda then. I'll put 'em in thee box and thee canst run away then.'

Now I can't say I needed a lot of persuading to do as she said. Her very presence, so strong a reminder of home and family, and the knowledge that they too were anxious to see me, stilled the small voice of conscience.

I wrote a little note to say that I was running away and put it beside the tea-caddy, where the woman would be bound to see it when she made the tea for my mistress.

The sight of the old lady nodding by the fire – her hands veined and thin as the claws of a plucked chicken – began to give me second thoughts. But she stirred and sharply ordered me to be back before dusk. I didn't answer. For a while, a little while, I could escape from servitude. I was going to see and touch my little sisters and brother, my Mam and Dad, and the dear familiar sights of home.

# Cheltenham Spa

I decided to get another job to better myself. This time it was in Cheltenham, that aristocrat of towns, where in the 1920s everybody who wasn't a servant was a somebody; including the snooty little pekes and pomeranians, creatures rated much higher in their mistresses' eyes than the servants.

Again I was to be the only maid, and still at five shillings a week, but I thought I was making headway into a more sohisticated and plentiful world. In fact, the only thing I found more plentiful was the work.

Although my new master had been among the sons of gentlemen at Cheltenham College, it had not managed to educate out of his nature a patronising distaste for servants, and all the 'lower orders'. Ironically, he had married 'beneath him' – a pretty, calculating nurse. She had thought the private-ward appendix patient was worth more than nursing, and after his discharge, she manipulated him into marriage.

They had both been 'had'. The business he had inherited on the death of his widowed mother had come to a poor pass under her mismanagement. But he and his wife shared the same snob values. She had married to get into the middle class – and by damned he *was* middle class – upper middle class old chap, actually. They were determined to cut some sort of figure, even if it was on very thin ice. The coming of their two children, a boy then three years old, and a girl of six months, had aggravated their situation.

They were in need of a strong young fool – one who could be house-maid from six till one for cleaning the house, then parlour-maid for waiting at table, then nanny for the children's afternoon outings, then washerwoman in the evenings. They needed a creature that would run on very little fuel and would not question her lot. Instead, they had me; but at any rate I *was* a fool.

I soon found my new mistress's sharp tongue a more efficient goad than my old one's walking-stick. I became quite a nimble worker, especially as, on the spartan diet she provided, I had no surplus flesh to hold me back.

Every Wednesday, after I had washed up the lunch things and cleared up the kitchen, I was free until ten o'clock. This arrangement held good for alternate Sundays too.

There were other girls from our small village working as maids in Cheltenham. One of these, Dolly, who had been a special friend at school and had shared my fourteenth birthday party, had taken the trouble to write to Mam for my address. Then she wrote to me, saying she would call for me on our next Sunday afternoon off; we could go to the pictures together.

My employers had taken their children off for the day, making a great deal of fuss piling into the rather grand car they could ill-afford to run. I had been given a long list of jobs to get through before I went out, and madam informed me she had left my lunch under a traycloth on the kitchen table. I tackled my jobs with a will, heartened by the thought of spending my afternoon off with Dolly. I was scrubbing the basement passage – the last of my chores – when she rang the door bell. It was half past two.

'I thought it was supposed to be your 'alf-day! I finished work at 'alf past twelve! My missus didn't even let me do the washing-up after dinner! You should finish work at one o'clock on your 'alf-day; it's the law.' These observations were made in a very loud voice, and with a jerk of the head upwards that implied 'and I 'ope them buggers upstairs be listenin'.'

'They be gone out for the day,' I told her. 'Never mind, I've only got to eat me dinner, and change; that wun't take me long.'

'It certainly wun't take thee long to yut thee dinner!' Dolly gasped, when she lifted the traycloth.

Rigor mortis had already begun to set in on the tiny cube of stale corned beef; the dry outside was curling up with mortification for having bothered a clean plate. Sitting in a lonely state on another plate was a wizened apple.

'What's that s'pos'ed to be, your 'ors d'urvies?'

'No, that's my dinner.'

'The old cow! Where do they kip the vittles 'ere?'

Before I could tell her where the larder was, and that it was locked, Dolly had discovered both.

'Not left you even a bit o' bread to fill up the carners! You shoulda' seen what I 'ad for my dinner. But I won't tell you; it'd be croo-el! Never mind; we'll go round and see my cousin Olive in her job afore we go to the pictures.'

Dolly's cousin, Olive, worked as a parlour-maid in a private boarding school for small boys. 'I 'ope it's cook's Sunday off. Miserable old faggot 'er is; don't like the maids 'avin' any friends in the kitchen.'

We were lucky; cook was out. The five maids on duty were just about to sit down to their tea, laid on one end of an enormous, well-scoured, wooden table. Each girl's plate was rationed to three thick slices of bread and marge, a dab of red jam, and a good-sized wedge of pale currant cake. The kitchen-maid poured out their tea, and a cup each for Dolly and me. I tried to look uninterested in the feast about to be consumed, but when Dolly realised a cup of tea was going to be our lot, she told them about my 'dinner' and what a 'starve-guts' job I had landed myself in. Five pairs of kindly sympathetic eyes gave me their full attention; and each took a bit of her cake and bread and jam and piled it on to a plate for me, saying what a shame it was.

It was too much; I burst out crying. I wasn't sure whom I was feeling sorriest for; myself – or those five kind girls, barely allowed their identities under the uniform caps and aprons.

I was too choked up to eat much, but they put their offerings in a paper bag, and insisted I took it with me. When we got outside I unjustly accused Dolly of letting me make a fool of myself.

It was heaven to go inside the warm dark picture house, where tear stains did not show. Here I could exchange my lot for one of the glamour queens of Hollywood. Afterwards I returned to reality, and said good night to Dolly. Cheltenham seemed an aloof and cold place to walk through.

Indoors again, I sat on the edge of the narrow iron bedstead that practically filled my tiny box-room, and ate the remains of my food parcel.

Every day, by breakfast time, I had done a couple of hours hard work. I had the appetite of a growing girl nearing fifteen years. My mistress bought my bacon separate from theirs; it was narrow streaky rashers cut very thin, and one of these was put out each morning for my breakfast. But, for my bread, I had to go into the dining-room. 'One, two, or three slices?' the master would ask, somehow implying by his manner that it was an act of charity to give me any. Sensing it to be grudged, I was too proud to ask for three, too hungry to stick at one. I always compromised, 'two, sir, please.'

Despite her toffee-nosed ambitions, or perhaps to show off her status, the mistress had remained friendly with one of her nursing colleagues. This was an exquisitely pretty young woman. I thought her pink-and-white complexion, and her golden-haired, blue-eyed beauty, must surely be the equal of Mary Pickford's. She looked as though butter wouldn't melt in her mouth. Once she came in her nurse's uniform, and I thought 'ministering angel' a very apt description. Sometimes she came to lunch; on these occasions the master gave her a lift to the house in his car.

One afternoon, the mistress was downstairs in the dining-room, and I was upstairs just completing my weekly turn-out of the lounge. Through the lace curtains I saw the master's car draw up, and him handing Nurse Hale out. Not wishing to emerge into the hall just as they were coming in, I waited in the lounge, and heard the front door quietly open and close. A little longer – for them to pass through – and I came out. But they were there! Very still, very quiet, and *very* close together!

In fact, it took them a whole minute to get unstuck from as passionate an embrace as ever Rod la Rocque and Vilma Banky could manage. I was shocked; so shocked you could have knocked me down with the feather duster I was carrying.

Fancy! The likes of her! So beautiful, so *nice*, wanting to be kissed by the likes of him – someone the likes of me would turn her nose up at – an ungentlemanly man in gentleman's clothes! I suppose he must have had considerable hidden charm, but I hadn't cottoned on to it.

By the colour of their faces, they had had a bigger shock than I. Oh well, their business was none of mine. Even my own wasn't, for when the master and mistress had been discussing me with visitors while I was still in the room, and I had ventured to correct them on a point, I had been told that servants didn't have eyes or ears for their betters' conversation and activities. So the surprised lovers went into the dining-room, and I went on with my work, and nothing was said.

The next morning, when I went in for my breakfast, I realised that the master's maxim about servants' eyes and ears was not strictly true. Instead of his usual enquiry, he gratuitously suggested I might like *three* slices of bread, *and* he gave me a big smile with the offer! I recognised the insinuated bribe with its suggestion that I might be capable of blackmail, and the tacit admission that he'd been aware of my hunger. I looked him coldly and squarely in the eye.

'No, thank you, two as usual, sir,' I replied; and the piece I went without was by far the most satisfying.

# On the Farm

Six months was the limit of my endurance as far as the Cheltenham household was concerned. I escaped to home as soon as I reasonably could, and determined never again to look for a job where my employers were trying to keep up an appearance beyond their means.

But as I couldn't stay for long to add to the burden of the little ones, I knew it could be only a brief respite.

After two pinch-belly jobs, the chance to work in the house of a remote hundred-acre farm in Wales seemed a good idea. It would be no progress moneywise; the wage offered was still only a pound a month, but 'farmhouse' surely meant bowls of big brown eggs, sizzling home-cured bacon, thick creamy butter on home-baked bread, and mugs full of frothy milk still warm from the cow.

It also meant being 'a strong willing girl'. Well, I was willing, and farmhouse food would make anyone strong, surely. Best of all, I shouldn't have to wear the hated caps and aprons, and I would sit down to meals with the family.

It was two miles to Little Rowan Farm from the nearest bus stop, but I only had to walk up the lane. My clothes were now packed in my new, large four-and-eleven cardboard portmanteau; it wasn't very heavy. The mud was the big hindrance; it was February. Recent snows had melted, and the red clay soil was a nice mud-pie consistency. I gathered enough on my shoes, and on my portmanteau when I put it down for a rest, to fill a fair-size window box.

There was still enough light for me to pick my way round to the back of the farmhouse. The front of the house was in darkness, and the porch door in the middle was obviously not for general use. I had already acquired the back-door entrance habit, anyway.

This back-door was a stable-fashioned one, with a separate top and bottom half. It was wide enough for a horse to get through. When the top half was opened at my knocking, I took in a picture of living, primitive even by my standards.

I looked in on a long, narrow room, ceilinged with black oak beams the size of a small tree. Where the dark shadows revealed them, the walls were distempered in ochre. A small window at the far end was covered with a roller blind to shut out the night. On an enormous table was a paraffin lamp. By its soft light, and the flickers from the hearth, I saw a few oak shelves, ebony black with age, arranged with odd cups, saucers, and plates. A crudely made settle, covered with shiny black oilcloth, was pushed up hard against the wall facing the fireplace. This fireplace was merely a cavernous hole in the wall, surrounded by slabs of stone. From a chain fixed to an iron bar hung a huge witch-type black cauldron. Half a small tree trunk sulked smokily in the middle of the fire, and a big black kettle stood just nudging the flame on the hearth.

The man half-dozing in a wooden armchair by the fire might have been John Bull himself. His eyes were closed, but one booted foot was gently tapping the rockers of a wooden cradle on the floor. The cherub baby in the cradle had the same bright ginger hair as himself.

A couple, obviously the baby's parents, sat with their backs to the door; between them a bag, for the feathers each was plucking from a chicken. In the wall, just above their heads, a little iron door marked the bread oven.

Just inside, and to my right, a boy about my own age was skinning one of a number of moles on the lid of a wash-copper built into the corner. His hands were like swedes.

In the opposite corner was a stone salting slab; above it, on the wall, hung the remains of a flitch of bacon covered with the grey salty rime that preserved it and protected it from flies. Here and there, on the stone-flagged floor, sacks were laid in strategic places to catch the dirt from muddy boots.

It wasn't a prepossessing place, yet its very ugly homeliness bore a comfort. I was sick of snobs.

I didn't feel uneasy to sit at the supper table with such people, but my notions of farmhouse food were knocked on the head at once. It was most unfortunate that I had an absolute abhorrence of cheese in any form. Supper at Little Rowan Farm was a choice – dry bread and cheese, or dry bread and broth from the cauldron, or dry bread and skim milk. It had one saving factor – the bread was unlimited. I chose broth with mine. This had plenty of pepper and salt in it, and a few bits of onion, easily seen floating in its pale grey slightly greasy depths. There was a faint flavour of bacon, but a vegetarian could have eaten it without much trouble to his conscience.

The others all had bread and cheese and cider. We didn't get up from the table until my new mistress (a fervent chapel-goer) had said grace. Privately, I told the Almighty that I didn't feel all that thankful, and my amen wasn't very enthusiastic.

After supper, with warm water from the kettle on the hearth, I washed up the supper things in a big chipped enamel bowl, after wiping the table down. Bert, the mole-skinner, showed me how to use the water pump in the back-yard. Then we fetched the milk-separator from the bitterly cold dairy. I gathered that I was supposed to be overawed by this newly acquired modern contraption. Buckets of milk were poured into the capacious top, and out of one spout came the cream, and from the other, thin bluish skim milk. The bowls of cream were taken into the dairy for butter making; the skim milk was for our domestic use, and for the animals.

By the next evening, I knew that the old man was the baby's paternal grandfather. He was a widower, and had five married sons and two married daughters. They all rented farms, and he stayed a little time with each one, applying his skill to helping them at hedging, haymaking, cider-making, mangel-chopping, and so on. He treated life like a fat, juicy steak, something to get stuck into, and, even at the age of seventy, any woman's behind that came within his reach was for slapping. Having him under her roof was torture to my Calvinistic, chapel-besotted, over-refined mistress. Only the obvious adoration that mother and grandfather felt for the baby made the arrangement possible.

Bert was another of his grandchildren, one of six orphaned by the death of their parents. He and his brothers and sisters had been shared out among the others; and my employers had certainly got a bargain.

From the age of nine, when they had taken him in, he'd been made to earn his keep by pre-school and after-school chores. Now he gave them full-time assistance, and didn't get a penny in wages. The only coppers he had to spend were the few odd ones he received for his moleskins.

While I was there, an act of parliament was passed, obliging his uncle to pay him a minimum of one pound a month. He never saw this money either; they banked it for him. And after that, the sight of Bert standing still for even a minute was hard for them to bear.

His body and soul were held together by the plainest of food; his clothes were patched-up cast-offs of his grandfather. The trousers' waist came nearly to his armpits, and the tattered matching jacket reached to his knees.

I had worn too many queer left-off garments myself to laugh at his comic appearance. My own shortage of working clothes was eased by a kind middle-aged woman who lived in a cottage up the lane. She gave me the dresses she'd worn as a VAD in the War. I was slim enough to hook up the twenty-inch waist, and tall enough for the skirts to come only to my ankles. They were made of stout khaki with brown trimming.

I had long hair tied back with a ribbon, and I was nearly sixteen years old. It was 1930, and the current fashions then were shingled or Eton-cropped hair, and short dresses showing fancy beribboned garters.

One autumn day, I nipped down the field in the hope of finding a walnut left under the tree in the corner. As I searched, a huntswoman rode up. She reined in her mount at the side of me, and in a loud, assured 'county' voice, called to a male rider a few yards away: 'Do come and have a look at this. Isn't it quaint?'

She stared at me with such insolent amusement that I realised I was the 'it' referred to. The blood rushed to my cheeks, but I stared back. Her heavily rouged and powdered face was covered with a black net attached to a hard black hat. She rode side-saddle, and her shining black boots were almost covered by a long black hobble skirt.

Talk about the pot calling the kettle black! She looked ridiculous, but I had better manners than to say so out loud. The man drew up and she repeated her remark.

'Beautiful, I'd say,' he observed, and touched his riding hat to me. Then he snubbed her further by bidding me good morning with a warm smile that was more than polite. 'Good mornin'' and good 'untin',' I replied. And to the disappearing back of his companion I wished, 'Good riddance, and I 'ope you come a cropper in some cow muck.'

For a few minutes a gentleman had made me feel like a lady.

I worked a year on that farm, and the dinners only varied by the nature of the potatoes – waxy in their early summer youth, floury the rest of the year. The swedes, boiled in a big iron saucepan, tasted always the same; and so did the home-cured bacon, sizzling in a heavy black pot next to the saucepan. Day in, day out, weekdays and Sundays, it was always the same, and it never tasted less than delicious. Hunger was a good appetiser, for our breakfast was always thick toast and margarine, with plenty of sweet tea.

Nothing that could be taken to the market on Tuesday was ever used at home. The cracked or soft-shell eggs were given to the men for breakfast. There were never enough dud eggs for Bert or me!

But this didn't worry Bert. Once he knew I could be trusted, he confided in me that when he found where the hens laid off, he just broke the shell and swallowed the eggs raw.

He was quite a sturdy lad, and I felt sorry for him. Sometimes, when I was doing some chore, and no one about, I let him put his arms round my waist, and maybe a hand would creep up and cup a breast. I had begun to feel a need to be caressed; but not by Bert. He wasn't my style at all.

When the master, mistress and baby went off with their wares in the pony and trap to market, I fed the ducks and fowls, did the cleaning, and cooked dinner for Bert, the old man, and myself. On market day we lingered a little longer over it, but one day, Bert had a lot to do and took himself off early.

The old man stretched out his legs, patted his round paunch, belched heartily, and with a wicked twinkle in his eye, suggested I forget the work and go up on the bed with him for a slap and a tickle. I thought the idea outrageously funny, and nearly fell about laughing, he wasn't my type either. The old bull stumped out, a bit aggrieved at my reaction.

Things like half-days off were never mentioned down on the farm; but I used to enjoy my weekly two-mile walk to the village shop. I didn't enjoy it so much on the way back, for a bag of tea, sugar, flour, and salt, plus a gallon tin of paraffin, took the dance out of my footsteps. I was quite a strong girl now, for if Bert had his egg bonus, I was a secret cream dipper every time I went into the dairy.

As I shut the farm gate behind me, and set off down the lane to the shop, my spirits rose. For the next hour or two, unsupervised by my mistress's sharp eye, I could belong to myself. The shopping bag and the paraffin can couldn't weigh down my spirits. Oh, lucky, lucky me! To be alive and sixteen years old, and walking up a Welsh country lane on a perfect May morning. Look near, look far, all was a transport of delight.

On the left was a tree-ringed pond with a couple of horses grazing. Close by stood two ancient oaks, no longer leaf-bearing, gnarled and distorted with sylvan senility; a regular granma and grancher of trees. Beyond them, in the far distance, the Sugar Loaf dominated a mountainous skyline. As I walked, I would note where the primrose clumps grew thickest on the banks. I could wheel the baby there later, and then pick and bunch them for market.

Mrs Jones was shaking her mats. 'Mornin', gal,' she called out cheerily. 'Indeed to G-o-d, this bit o' sun shows up the cobwebs. Mind you step in for a cup o'tea on your way back, look. Be a good gal, and bring me a tin of Nestlé's milk. Tell Dai I'll pay 'im Friday.' On an after-thought, 'and two Oxos to make the gravy look as if it's got a bit o' meat in it.'

Yes, Mrs Jones, righto, Mrs Jones! Anything to oblige Mrs Jones! It was that sort of a morning, anyone would have obliged anybody for anything.

A farm labourer on a bicycle passed me: 'Mornin', my lovely,' he beamed; he too had got the mood of the day. I heard Mrs Jones call out to him, 'How are you getting on now, Gwillum?'

'Not very often; the old gal won't let me!'

In broad daylight, rabbits turned the land into a conjuror's hat, appearing by magic, and disappearing again after short ecstatic sessions of grass nibbling. They wagged their rounded powder-puff behinds in careless defiance of their enemies.

To the shop I trod the light fantastic; but homeward was a plod, weighed down as I was by my load. I was thankful indeed to reach Mrs Jones's.

Apart from her big black-leaded grate, I can't recall anything special about the dark brown inside of her cottage. But I do remember the Welsh cakes she gave me with a cup of tea – flat, round, currant-sprinkled, melt-in-the-mouth morsels, tasting then like manna from heaven. We had an unspoken agreement not to mention these stops for refreshment to my mistress; and my load seemed lighter for the rest of the way.

'There's a time you've been,' my mistress would say tartly. 'I thought you'd forgot yourself and gone to Abergavenny by mistake! Well, fill the lamps, and then you'd better get on straight away peeling the swedes and potatoes for dinner. You won't have time now to scrub out the dairy first.' I never minded her scolding; I felt sorry for her. She hadn't enjoyed the glory of my four-mile walk.

Long before I picked primroses for market, I was put gathering snowdrops, even the first few hardy ones that peeped up through the snow here and there. They were one penny a bunch, and cheap at the price if you took into account the aches I suffered as my frozen fingers thawed. But the sheer joy of gathering wild flowers made up for it.

Because of our simple diet, only onions were grown in the vegetable garden; potatoes came from the field. But there were also a few gooseberry bushes. I didn't expect to get any of these cooked, but I did look forward to eating a few ripe ones. I was disappointed. The mistress shared the job of picking them – again for market – with me, and somehow, under her forbidding eye, I didn't have the nerve to pop one into my mouth.

However, I made up for it with apples. Bert and the master gathered these, and stacked them in a huge mound on the flagstones by the back door, while they waited their turn to borrow the cider press.

Old Fagin himself couldn't have criticised the sly speed with which I pinched a few on my way to the privy. I knew the pale greeny-yellow ones that were sugar-sweet and juicy.

At first, my extra calls of nature were shams, just simply to sit enthroned in the privy, juicily munching and watching the tell-tale cores float out of sight down the stream. But after the apples had been there a week, I had to dash down the garden path in earnest, too quickly to bend and snatch one up.

'I see you got the back-door trot; perhaps you should eat a few green apples to have a good clear-out,' Bert sniggered in my ear.

I had my own back on him later. Myfanwy, the postgirl, brought our letters on horseback. She was nineteen and very good-looking, and seemed to me like a member of royalty, sitting up there so casual and at ease.

We saw her only rarely, and then usually with my letter from Mam. Bert told me enviously he had never had a letter in his life. I bided my time and wrote him one. I wrote it backwards so that he would have to hold it up to the mirror to read. I wrote, 'Important message under stamp on envelope – tell no one – a secret admirer.' Under the stamp I printed, 'April Fool.'

On April the first, when he and the master came in for dinner, I gave Bert the letter. I regretted it the moment I saw the joy and excitement it caused him. His piled-up plate of dinner was usually the highlight of his day, but it got cold while he painstakingly made out the writing in a piece of old spotted mirror by the door. Then gently, after licking the stamp wet with his tongue, he carefully peeled it off, not noticing there was no postmark. I wished I hadn't seen the hurt, and the dreadful disappointment in his face, when he got the message. I was as near to tears for my tactless cruelty as he was, but I couldn't rub in his humiliation by showing my pity.

That summer, the hay had been cut and turned by pitchfork over and over to sun-dried perfection. The master had the countryman's feel that rain was on the way. Could the mistress spare me to help him and Bert get the hay into the rick?

I was careful not to let her see how much I would love to go. I even scowled to put her off the scent. She seemed to think that, in Heaven's name, life must be a cross to bear, not something to make light of. Humming and hawing a bit, she agreed, reluctantly.

The master let me climb into the waggon behind old Bonnie, the carthorse, whose back was wide enough to dance a hornpipe on. She made nothing of getting up the short steep bank to the gate of the meadow. Bert swung the gate open, and immediately we were at work.

Now it was my job to level off and tread down the forkfuls of hay that the master and Bert loaded from either side. In no time at all, all of us except Bonnie were sweating profusely. The men could strip to their shirts, but not take them off, with such a mistress in charge.

I, of course, had to sweat it out in my ankle-length old VAD dress, but at least I had the sleeves rolled up above the elbows. I didn't care anyway; it was lovely to be out.

The master said I was doing the job as well as any man. High praise, indeed, for when she was about, he was almost as dumb as Buster Keaton.

He and Bert kept pitching up the hay, and I kept treading it down. The load got higher and higher. The ground seemed a perilous way off, especially when the top-heavy load swayed as Bonnie got on uneven ground. Eventually I was using a pitchfork to take it from the loaders who could no longer reach. But, at last, when I was letting out little squeals of apprehension, the master and Bert threw ropes up to me to let down the other side and secure the load. There was no way for me to get down until we got to the rick and the ladder. While the men had a pause and put on their jackets, I sat, queen of all I surveyed, on a throne of golden hay, crowned with a red-spotted hankerchief corner-knotted. As far as the eye could see, my pastoral domain was of exceeding beauty.

However, my regal dignity was sorely tried as Bonnie gingerly felt her way down the steep slope from meadow to lane. Talk about Cleopatra on a camel! It couldn't have been a bumpier ride. The master looked happy and quite boyish, as he laughed up to reassure me I was safe.

We felt a spot or two of rain; getting that hay in so neatly on time quite went to the master's head. When the waggon got to the rick, he told me to step off the top on to the hay that was already stacked there, and wait while Bert and he unloaded. I could have a little rest up there. I caught on when they took away Bonnie, and the empty waggon, *and* the ladder. I was stranded.

'There's plenty o' rats in that stack to keep you company,' guffawed Bert, 'there's nothing they like better than running up women's skirts.'

'That's how she shoulda' trod that hay down on the waggon,' laughed the master, as I jumped up and down like Nijinsky, and screamed with panic.

The noise brought the mistress out; the grins dropped from their faces, and with a show of serious concern they placed the ladder against the stack. But the mistress had her suspicions. She stood there, while they turned their backs to me as I descended, though the length of my skirt was modest enough. I followed her indoors, turning behind her back to poke my tongue out at the miscreants. I guessed the master was in the doghouse for a bit.

Nature had been trying hard to push me into womanhood, and she was having a bit of a struggle. Now, after half a year on the farm, she was eventually winning. A frugal but healthy diet, plenty of exercise, sound sleep, early rising, early bed, no worries, and the fresh air from the mountains filling the lungs by day and night. It had its effect; I was blossoming out very roundly in the right places: a fact that, unknown to me, hadn't escaped the watchful eye of the young man who owned the next farm. He had even wasted his time hanging about on his land next to the lane, to watch me on my weekly walk to the shop.

If his name cropped up at the farm, my mistress gave a disapproving sniff, for he was known as 'a bit of a wild lad' who rode a motorbike, and stayed out half the night in Abergavenny town. He was twenty-six.

I had been allowed to go into Abergavenny once for a spending spree, with three months' saved-up wages. I sent a postal order home to Mam, and had plenty left for shoes and a few everyday clothes, plus a pale-green silk dress and a wide-brimmed lacy straw hat with green ribbons. When the year was up, and I due for a holiday, I intended to impress the boys back home. Then an unexpected opportunity came for me to wear my new finery.

Two things happened. The old man went off to stay with another son, and the new chapel minister invited my master and mistress to stay on after Sunday evening service, and to take supper with him.

These blessings put my mistress in such a transport of good humour that she told me I could have some time off to go to Sunday-evening chapel. Poor Bert would have to be the Christian who did all the chores! 'Six days shalt thou labour' had to be overlooked in his case.

Normally, I'd have preferred to stay at home and help Bert rather than listen to a Sunday sermon, but I wasn't going to miss the chance to try out my new clothes. Saturday morning I washed my hair and put it in curling papers.

The master and mistress, with the baby, started for chapel well ahead of me, which gave me the chance to pinch a dab of her Pond's Vanishing Cream to put on my snub nose. As I looked in her mirror, I blushed rose-pink with pleasure. Oh, it couldn't be me! That pretty girl, in a lovely dress, with brown silky curls, and round face framed in lacy straw!

Bert was so surprised he nearly stepped back into the bucket of pig-swill he'd been stirring. He looked quite hungry at the sight of me.

Freedom to walk out in the hedgerowed lane normally meant that I would indulge in a hop-skip-and-dance routine when out of sight of the farm. But today I walked proud and sedate like a young lady of quality.

On the very corner of the lane was a farmhouse that looked in the front as grand as a manor, although the back was the usual quagmire surrounded by barns, stables, and pig-styes. Just as I passed, a girl about my own age picked her way carefully to the gate. She was carrying a Bible, and was obviously in her Sunday clothes. Not having seen her before, I didn't venture to speak. She, however, had seen me often as I carried the paraffin, and knew that I was the 'help' at Little Rowan Farm. She did similar work on a grander scale. She was Welsh and friendly, and talkative. Her dad was a miner too, in Abertillery. She was the eldest of six, and her name was Letty Meadows. We had a lot in common, except that I thought her name and herself much prettier than I.

The chapel was a mile further on past the village. It was a minute building of grey stone, not important enough to have its own churchyard, but set in a neat grass plot just off the road. It was almost filled. Considering the sparseness of the local population, it proved how popular chapel attending was in Wales.

The service had not yet begun. My master and mistress were up front, talking to the new minister. Filled with gracious superiority by the minister's attention, my mistress beckoned me to her and introduced me as 'our maid'. I thought the description savoured of swank, and wasn't in the spirit of Jesus as taught in chapel. I was glad to return to Letty on the back seat by the door.

She was no more interested in the sermon than I was; neither were a couple of likeable-looking lads, in the seat in front of us, who weren't taken in by the apparent indifference Letty and I showed to their head-turnings in our direction.

'I wonder if they'll follow us after,' whispered Letty hopefully.

In unspoken agreement, we didn't hang around the chapel door, but hurried off down the road, to escape surveillance by our elders.

'Don't turn round, but, indeed, they are following us,' said Letty, well pleased.

Gauche and unsure like dog puppies, bold and diffident by turns, they whistled the popular love ballads of the day to us, and shouted out compliments disguised as sarcasm.

We answered and encouraged them in the only ways we knew – tossing our curls, giggling to each other, and even looking round to acknowledge their presence. Suddenly, a tuppenny bar of chocolate fell, from mid-air, in front of our feet.

'Which one do you like best?' asked Letty. Highly flattered at getting any masculine attention at all, I didn't feel too fussy; also it was most likely that they were both after Letty. So, to be on the safe side, I lied, 'I don't fancy either of 'em.'

After about half a mile, the boys had got up to within a few feet of us; but they hung back a bit when they saw our neighbour farmer waiting at the kerbside with his motorbike. Much to my surprise, he started to push his motorbike, and walk alongside us. Surprise is not a strong enough word for what I felt when he asked *me* if I would take a pillion lift home. I could only suppose that he didn't have the nerve to ask Letty. She was so much prettier than I, and I then judged feminine attraction simply by the face.

I was not enamoured of mine. 'More like a Chink's dial!' I used to scold my reflection – high cheekbones, squat nose, wide mouth. That I had grown to five feet six inches tall, with a tiny waist, and lovely feminine proportions had quite escaped my notice. If I sound immodest, it's because I saw, many years later, some snapshots taken at the time. And if a modern sixteen-year-old miss thinks I was ludicrously retarded, I *was*.

'Take Letty instead,' I offered haughtily, for I wanted none of his charity.

'There isn't room for the two of you, and it's you I asked,' he said firmly, and quickly added, with some tact, 'Letty hasn't so far to go as you.'

'Go on, gal, have a ride,' urged Letty. I was so convinced of Letty's superiority, there was no need to feel pity for any slight, even unintended. Anyway, she had the two beaux behind her to choose from. I was also inwardly excited beyond measure at such a turn of events. So I couldn't resist accepting my moment of glory.

I took off my hat, and sat as gracefully as I could on the pillion. My heart was in my mouth, for more than one reason, when the motorbike chugged into life.

When we turned off the main road into the lane, the ride became very bumpy; but as soon as he got to the first gate on his land, he stopped and wheeled the bike inside. 'I'd like to walk you home the rest of the way,' he said.

At first he politely left a stranger's gap, bridged by mutual physical awareness between us; but suddenly, on pretext of an imaginary stumble, he took my arm. The pressure of his strong hand, firm yet gentle, pretending to hold me up, was very pleasing. But I was unpractised in coquetry, and it took nearly half a mile more before his arm got round my shoulder, with my head gently pressed against his chest.

The strong curve of a man's right arm is surely the dearest haven for a woman's head. By the time we had reached the horse-chestnut tree in the lane opposite Little Rowan, his arm had got down round my waist.

My instinctive woman's guile had been awakened during our walk, and I made a show of reluctance when he suggested we sit down under the chestnut tree. But slowly I allowed his tender male dominance to persuade me, and we were on the soft grass, he with his back against the trunk. Now I felt as helpless as a seedling that cannot resist the lure of the sun, forced by the very basis of its nature to grow, to bloom, and to seed.

I let the young man take me in his arms, tilt my unresisting face to his, gently brush my lips with his, searching for, and finding for both of us, such a profound sweetness as I had never dreamed of. Everything beautiful I had ever known, or thought of, had lain dormant for this moment, to be awakened in this kiss. A kind of reverence came over us.

I could feel the pounding of my heart and his. It was just a kiss – no more. But for me, new to the taste of love, it was enough, more than enough. The young man pulled me to my feet, and even the touching of our hands was ecstasy, and unabated till we reached the porch. Then, tenderly, as though I were made of gossamer, the young farmer kissed my lips, my forehead, and my work-roughened hands. 'I'll watch for you,' he whispered, and was gone.

It seemed as if I floated round to the back-door. I wanted no supper. The cream pan did not tempt me to dip a finger. I could live without bread and drink tonight, for I had tasted nectar. I was sixteen and I *had* been kissed.

But Bert, poor Bert, still a clod-hopping mortal, *he* needed some supper.

I was coming out of the dairy with the cheese for him when he clumped in through the door.

'*I* saw who brought you home tonight.' His voice sounded dour and accusing. 'When he realised I'd spotted him, he told me not to tell my uncle.'

He told him not to tell his uncle! One minute I had been floating on the airy pinnacle of ecstasy, a Venus adored, and now I was the disowned beggar-maid, someone ashamed to have been seen with.

To have been escorted to the door of the Kingdom of Love, to have had my hand kissed like a queen, and then to have been snubbed so, and snubbed in front of someone like Bert!

At sixteen, black was black and white was white; it took years to merge them into grey. Lover to traitor, nectar to dust, I was still too full up for any supper. For now I was stuffed up with outraged feminine pride. By the time I got to bed it was overflowing from my eyes in two salty torrents.

Hitherto I had loved to waken in the morning to the pungent farmyard odours flavouring the new morning air, air that had come across the sea and over the top of the Sugar Loaf mountain. The soft feather bed did not compete too strongly with the new day beckoning through the window.

The waking sounds of birds and beasts, already heralded by the cock-crows near and far, gave importance to each day.

Come on, then, fowls! Fly from your perches, gobble up your scattered breakfast of golden corn.

Lumber ungainly up the lane, you cows, through the creaking, five-barred, wooden gate, into the rested field.

Don't wag your tail right off, old sheep dog, just because you are being let off your chain to manage, almost on your own, the moving of a hundred silly old sheep. Good dog, yes you *are* a good dog.

Stop your scolding quack-quack, you upstart ducks. I've got a lot of other jobs before I come to pull up the door of your pen.

Skinny sinuous cats, which of you were fighting like two Lucifers in the night? More ratting, and less tomming, you jealous Romeos. But here's your milk, all half a bucket of it, skimmed of course, to share between the six, seven, eight, oh, the lot of you.

There, I've seen to you all, but my heart's not in it any more; it's lying like lead in my side, and nobody knows, and nobody cares. I wish I was a cat, a sheep, a cow or a duck, you are somebody. I'm nobody, a proper nothing. No, I *am* a somebody; I'm Polly Mason, and I'll show him, oh, I'll show him! I'll walk by him, haughtier than any queen, if I ever set eyes on him again.

Set eyes on him again? Well, of all the cruel nerve! There he was, talking to the master by the granary door, and I must pass them to fetch some wood from the stack near the dog's kennel. I concentrated as much venom into the look I gave him as I then knew how to muster.

I threw the wood on the fire with enough angry carelessness to wake the baby, morning-napping in the wooden cradle on the floor. This brought me a sharp reprimand from the mistress to watch what I was doing.

I thought my master and mistress looked at me a bit quizzical when we were eating our dinner, but they made no comment on my behaviour.

It had not been the habit of the young farmer to call on my master, but now, to my annoyance and embarrassment, I could not help seeing them talking on several occasions. Once I was unlucky enough to answer the door to his knock. Luckily, the mistress was in the kitchen, for he held out his arms as though he would grab hold of me, and his eyes were as soft and begging as a spaniel's.

Let him do his underhand begging; I would not give him a bone if he were starving. I took great care to make myself scarce, and never to glance in his direction when he was about.

The village shop now delivered by van; I was half-glad, half-sorry that my weekly errand was finished. The exhilaration of feeling free for an hour or so was shadowed by the thought that I might bump into *him*.

It was a very cold autumn day when the shopkeeper forgot to bring our paraffin. We needed it for the lamps; I must put a move on with my chores and fetch it before dark.

On the way, I saw the cause of my misery walking behind a horse-drawn plough on his land some fields away. Away from the busy bustle of the farm, a deep sense of melancholy came over me. I would have to go away. I resolved to give in a month's notice the next day.

Hurrying home, changing the heavy can from one hand to the other to speed my progress, I was brought to a heart-pounding halt by the young farmer. He had been waiting behind the hedge near the last gate that bounded his land. He had stepped out in front of me and stood barring my way. Though already rosy-cheeked from exertion, I felt the blood rush to my face, and away from my legs.

I tried to side-step and pass him; I wanted none of his hole-in-the-corner attentions. With sheer strength he took the paraffin can from me, put an iron-grip on each of my shoulders, and backed me towards the gate. His manner was desperate and beseeching.

'Why do you keep hiding and turning away from me?' he begged, holding me in his arms against my will, and trying to find my lips with his.

Had I been a girl of true spirit I would have smacked his face and told him I was as good as he; and if he could not acknowledge openly he found me attractive, he could keep the secret all to himself.

Up till then my life had not done much to nurture such a spirit. I was full of inward pride, the sort that would cut off its nose to spite its face; the sort of pride that made a great fuss over the little it had to be proud about. I could not bear to put into words that hurt his slight had caused me. A week before, his kiss had made my body melt, yet now I felt as unyielding and unfeeling as the gate I was pressed against.

Puzzled and upset by my obstinacy, his ardour turned to anger; he let me go and walked back through the gate.

My mistress did not seem unduly upset when I gave her my month's notice. Though willing, I was not a particularly able servant. I found watching the floating myriads of dust particles highlighted in a shaft of sunlight through the window more amusing than polishing it off the furniture. Besides, I was getting a big girl with a big appetite; I was gone sixteen years old, and might be wanting a rise soon on my five-shilling-a-week wages. A livelier fourteen-year-old girl might be cheaper and easier to train.

I wrote home and told them I was leaving my job. Mam told a neighbour, and the neighbour put this item of news in her letter to her daughter who was working in London. By this means, before I had left the farm I had a letter from my neighbour's daughter telling me she could get me a job any time. It would be working for Jewish people, as she was, and the wages were very good, ten shillings a week, and they did not mind if you did not wear caps and aprons. Her address was in Aldgate.

Supper was eaten in high good humour the evening before I left the farm. Bert and the master had taken all day to walk some bullocks into Abergavenny for sale, and they had fetched a very good price. Bert was as high and mighty as the Prince of Wales, with a new cap the guv'nor had bought him, and the master and mistress were oozing with good humour.

'We did wonder a while back,' smiled the master, winking at his wife, 'if we were going to have you for a neighbour in time. Poor Dai took a proper fancy to you, you know, neglecting his own place, finding excuses to come across to see me. I knew who he'd *really* come to see. Mind you, he asked me all above board if it would be all right for him to take you out. I could tell by the way you looked at him he wasn't going to have any luck. You could have done worse, you know. There's many a girl round here would jump at the chance of him.'

The piece of broth-soaked bread I had just spooned into my mouth waited there to be swallowed; to go down with the surprise, the shame, the remorse and helplessness I felt trying to cope with the multiplicity of emotions these remarks had waked.

What an upstart! What an intolerant misjudger of character! What a fool I had been!

I like to think that if I had been a free agent, I would have jumped up from the table and run to make some apology. It is self-delusion. I had not the grace of character, the wit, or the experience to handle the situation. I had burned my boats, and I had fallen out of love. All the same I took remorse to bed with me that night, and it allowed me very little sleep.

The next morning I could have started my homeward journey early by catching a bus in the village. My mistress suggested I might help out until after dinner, and then catch a bus from a different direction. Instead of going down the lane, it would mean a walk of about three miles through a part of the surrounding countryside I had not seen. The master could give me explicit directions. It seemed a reasonable request, and I willingly agreed.

She put me to clean out all the fowls' cotes, and I worked at it like a Trojan. I shovelled up their droppings from the wooden floors into a wheelbarrow to heap in a corner of the garden. Then I pumped buckets of water, added some Jeyes' fluid, and sloshed out the cotes, perches, walls and floors.

By dinner-time I was having a proper farmer's farewell. I had muck up to the eyebrows, and my old working clothes and shoes stank of it. When I had washed and changed for my leave-taking, I rolled them up in a soiled pinafore and squeezed them down by my other clothes in my case.

I felt very little tugging at the heart-strings when I turned my back on Little Rowan Farm. The beautiful baby, now able to toddle from chair to chair, would hardly miss me, for I had been allowed little time to nurse or play with her.

The master came into the lane to point out the directions. I thanked him, waved goodbye to my mistress and the baby over the gate, and shouted 'cheerio' to Bert who was off up the lane to some chore in a field.

The weather was not dry underfoot. It rarely is in autumn, but the fields had nearly all been grazed, so the damp grass was short. The air was clean and sharp, just right for a long walk.

There is a great luxury being in open country all by oneself. I had hurried enough to put down my case, and rest against the knotty trunk of one of the trees; then I took a sort of mental bath in the tranquillity of it all. I could see sheep and cows in some distant fields, so I reckoned the farm which I had been told to pass would soon be in sight.

And so it was, the house almost hidden among its old barns. The only signs of life were the busy scratching hens close to the farm, a few geese a little further afield, and some pigs snuffling and grunting in a small fenced enclosure. Then a chained farm dog must have scented my coming on the wind. Strangers to bark at must have been a luxury, for he appeared to intend alerting the whole district by his yelping, snapping frenzy and straining at his chain. It made me quite nervous.

So, instead of going on to the forecourt of the farmhouse to get on to the path, I thought I would get out through the field-gate.

That field-gate was obviously the way the cows were taken in and out, too. Each side of it, the ground was churned up into a deep quagmire of mud and cowpats. It was impossible to open the gate without going through the mud; the overgrown hedges were not negotiable either.

Nature's commonsense department must have temporarily run out of stock when I was fashioned. I never thought of taking out from my case my already muddy farm shoes. I kept my best ones on, thinking that by a mad dash and a jump on to the barred gate I could skim the mud without getting really involved with it.

I did have the foresight to throw my case over the hedge first. A sharp run, and I was brought to a halt ankle-deep in mud so sticky it sucked my shoes under, and I stepped out into the morass in my stockinged feet. Well, I was not going to leave the shoes behind; they were brand-new and had cost me nine-and-eleven. I fumbled about for them in the glutinous mud, getting lots on my coat as well as my hands, to rescue them. Then I squelched on until I had fastened the gate behind me, and went to my case.

The catch had come undone from the bump it had got. After cleaning myself up as best I could, I changed my stockings. I put my old farm shoes back on; a lot of the dirt from them was now on the soiled clothes I had wrapped them in. Then I wrapped up my muddier new ones the same way. The case catch was very obstinate after my ill-treatment, but at last I got it to click into place.

I had not yet reached the status of owning a handbag, let alone a mirror, but I did not think I looked too bad. Nobody much would notice my feet on the bus, and the mud on my coat might be dry before then.

There was the path, anyway, leading down a steep hill. In places it was quite tricky negotiating the downward path with a case, but presently my concentration was broken by a living fire of beauty to my right. On the sides of a large natural gorge, trees of many varieties had taken root through the years. Unnaturally sheltered from the wind, they had retained their leaves very late, and the slanting rays of the sun burnished what was already a breathtaking feast for the eye. I stood and worshipped the vista, and felt the inadequate loneliness of the human spirit when faced with something it cannot measure up to.

The case resting against my leg reminded me I had a bus to catch. Goodbye, goodbye, beautiful lonely place!

I made it to the lane at the bottom of the path in nimble good time. Opposite was another farmhouse, much smaller than the previous one I had passed. A kindly-looking middle-aged man was sitting on a tree stump, just inside the gate, chopping pointed ends to hedge stakes. A gentle word to the collie sitting by his feet restricted it to a mere attempt to wag its tail.

It seemed a suitable opportunity to ask the time and how much further it was to the main road, where I hoped to catch the bus to Monmouth. He pulled out his pocket-watch on the end of its chain, and appeared to make some mental calculation.

'You've got nine minutes left, my gal; you'll have to step it out sharp, there isn't a minute to spare. Mrs Morris lives just a few yards up the main road, she'll tell you if the bus is gone.'

The man had looked a bit like my Dad, and this reminded me with a joyful rush that I was going home. Step it out? Yes, indeed I could, or even run, case and all. I did not intend to miss that bus.

I could not have imagined that man rushing to catch a bus anywhere. Farms seemed like self-contained islands bounded by their own hedgerows, miniature universes, no relation to the far-off busy cities that could have been on another planet.

I emerged on to the road just in time to wave the bus down as it was going past. A bit out of puff, I clambered on. There were two empty seats, one at the back, and one right up the front. The back one by the door would suit me fine; with the bus so full I would have to put my case up on the rack. In my thoughtless excitement I lifted it upside down, the catch flew open, and the back-seat passengers got a shower of the contents.

One of my muddy shoes hit a small boy on the side of the head; he opened his mouth to cry, but forgot his intention watching my mortified retrieving of a pair of muddy bloomers from a man's bald head; and the mad grabs I made to stuff such an unladylike cascade of belongings back into my case.

The bus door was shut, and the bus already moving, or I might have jumped off and thrown myself under it. Mustering no dignity whatsoever, I took my case to the seat at the front of the bus, and squeezed in with it somehow.

Certain that I was the object of contemptuous surprise, or at the best, pity, I could only pray that all my fellow passengers would stay on at Monmouth, and only I would have to change to the bus going to Cinderford. I was not quite lucky; two witnesses of my humiliation got on the Cinderford bus, and they travelled on when I alighted at the bottom of our village.

Nothing mattered now. I was back on familiar ground, back to my own identity, back among the friendly people of home.

'Well, well, 'tis Polly, ben't it? I s'pose thee bist wum for a 'oliday, my wench?' said Granny Herbert.

'No, I've left me job. Joy Barker a' got me a job in London not far from 'er.'

'Well, I 'eard as thee wast workin' on a farm, and seems thee'st brought a fair bit on it wum with thee.'

'That's nothin',' I bragged, still not knowing about my mud-smudged face, 'you should see what I've got in my case.' Oh, how funny it was now, in the telling to Granny Herbert.

'Thee bist a cough drop sure enough,' she chortled, 'come thee on in an' 'ave a cup o'tay.'

I shook my head.

I had not been able to write Mam what time to expect me, but my feet itched to get up the hill to home. I felt I could already smell the special tarts Mam would have made for my homecoming, and see the little ones, on their best behaviour, sitting patiently, or running to the gate to see if our Poll was coming, so that tea could at last begin.

# London Again

After three years in service, feeling now a woman of the world, I was more sensibly resigned to my lot.

Though I could not quite manage to leave the little ones and my loved surroundings dry-eyed – there was compensation in the feeling of excitement wondering what was in store for me in my new job in Aldgate.

Very much was in store for me! Without crossing the water I seemed to have landed in a fascinating foreign world where living was punctuated by exclamation marks. 'Such a bargain!' 'Such a shmatte!' 'Such a vedding!' 'Such a gefilte fish!' 'Such a shiksa I got now!' A place of 'eins's, zwei's, drei's, vier's and fünf's'. A way of life where Momma was indeed the queen of the gas stove and the preparing and cooking of food for her 'children' was the holy rite of her life.

'Taste, Vinnie, taste!' Borsht soup and gefilte fish, noodle soup and strudel – salt beef – and farfel pudding, chopped liver with hard-boiled eggs and onion served piled up on matza biscuits. We Christians can get our salivary juices running with the smell from a fish and chip shop – but oh there is an ocean's difference in that fish and the dish of fried cutlets Momma cooked for Shabbes.

Only the freshest, firmest, finest fish would do for her, and only the best Rakusens frying oil to cook them in – brought by long practice to the exact right sizzling temperature. Oh those plump forefingers of hers, prodding the endless supply of fish and chickens on the innumerable stalls down Petticoat Lane. If only the breath that was wasted in arguments with foregone conclusions as to the proper price for wares offered could have been caught and bottled!

Meat was meat (until all that koshering business of soaking it in water and salt had emasculated it) and milk was milk, but if they partook of one they must not partake of the other until four hours had elapsed. Never the twain must meet, nor even the dishes they were served on. The meat ones were kept in the scullery – milk ones on the dresser that took up one wall of the big kitchen. Washing-up was done in two separate bowls – if one had so much as caught sight of the other both would have been excommunicated to the dustbin.

The standards of hygiene in that Jewish household could have passed in an operating theatre. Some of their fastidious habits rubbed off on to me and remain with me forty years later.

I ate most of my meals from the large kitchen table with the family. Shabbes was the exception. The thirty bentwood chairs round the massive table in the dining-room were often inadequate to seat the tribe of relatives who came to nosh the salt herrings with onion rings, gefilte fish topped with boiled carrot, hard-boiled eggs, salad and fruit. Fish, fruit and water – or lemon tea – occupied the no-man's-land between milk and meat so no one had to fast four hours if they didn't want to. Apart from plenty of silver candlesticks to hold the candles lit for the Shabbes there was little in the way of ornaments – just as well for they would have come a cropper with all the pantomime of gestures that accompanied the conversation and laughter. As the visitors kept piling down the basement stairs to the dining-room, greeting each other with 'good Shabbes', all I could say under my breath was 'good riddance' – the washing-up seemed endless.

When was a domestic servant not a domestic servant? When I was the shiksa in that Jewish household. I was not expected to wear cap and apron – I shared a bedroom with daughters Leah and Becky until Leah married – leaving late-born Becky, aged eleven, the only unmarried daughter. If the family were talking in English on non-personal matters I was allowed to chip in with my say. In the workshops that occupied the two top floors of the house, the sons, daughters and in-laws provided most of the work force, for Momma had produced seven children to go with the three already born to the widower she had married. When business was good they would work fifteen hours a day – and I worked fifteen hours a day for their domestic comfort.

I had practically no time off except to be a chaperon companion to Becky when she went to the pictures. Dear beautiful little Becky – she came to treat me like an older sister and I only had to tell her how I would love to see a picture and she made sure I did. When the summer heat drew out the bugs from the walls – despite all the spirits of salt Momma made me paint in the crevices of the iron bedsteads – they got on the snowy-white duvets. Becky and I would have penny bets on a couple of bugs as to which would reach the highest point of the wall first, then fell asleep before finding out.

Once when I received a letter from home containing the sad news of the death of a childhood friend, I was distraught with grief and could not hide it. Instead of eating my breakfast (which I took with Momma when the family had gone up to the factory or off to school) I wept into it. Momma couldn't read or write, but between my gulps she begged me to tell her what was the matter. The tears came in her own eyes, and as an older friend to younger friend she told me about the death of a little sister of hers many years ago which still grieved her. She let the work go and shared and halved my sorrow with me. She was my mistress and my employer – but such a universal mother was she that I could not help feeling she was also a bit of a Momma to me.

I learnt to hold on to my ten shillings wages as grimly as Scrooge, for Leah was always trying to sell me a bargain. Mind you, I learnt this lesson painfully. It was when Leah beguiled me into buying a pair of her high-heeled upper-crust-style size four-and-a-half shoes for my plebeian broad size six feet. Somehow I managed to squeeze into them, and like a pig on stilts I hobbled in conceited agony trying to keep pace with Becky on the way to the Brick Lane Palace cinema. As soon as we were in our seats I took off my shoes for the comforting freedom of a carpet of peanut shells, cool orange peel and sweet wrappings. The ugly sisters stood as much chance of getting into Cinderella's glass slipper as I had of getting my swollen inflamed feet back into Leah's left-offs. I hadn't got into the habit of buying silk stockings so it was barefoot through the streets for me – my feet feeling as conspicuous and big as Darling Clementine's!

'Serve you right,' Becky scolded me. 'You ought to know by now that Leah could sell a side of bacon to a Rabbi if she put her mind to it.'

Leah was forced to give me up as a customer for her clothes – she was very slim and determined to remain so despite Momma's hysterical wailings at the sight of what Leah left on her piled-up plate. Momma extracted some comfort piling all the family's left-overs on to my plate. Leah remained slim – I grew plump. Leah just had to admit that 'it didn't quite fit' when I stood, arms in a rigid back stretch position unable to reach upwards or forwards, a six-inch gap between buttons and buttonholes on a coat she was trying to flog me for a week's wages. Once in the cause of high fashion Leah did manage to get a quart into a pint pot. It was when she got married and was determined to make her short fat Momma look elegant for once. This meant strait-jacketing Momma into a corset at least two sizes too small. It took four of us to pummel and push small mountains of adipose tissue inside a few hooks and eyes at the top – only to cause it to burst out when we fastened the ones at the bottom. Poor Momma – in the couple of hours it took us to get that corset fastened up she had groaned and sweated pounds away under the strain – we were a bit slimmer ourselves too.

'I'm dying,' she gasped when Leah had finished dressing her in a fashionable outfit in which she was cruelly uncomfortable. Momma survived the wedding day – but it must have nearly killed her having no room for the grand nosh-up after the ceremony.

The three unmarried sons were nice decent young men – but they could not resist my new voluptuous curves for a bit of free pinching practice. Of course, young Jews must not take a surreptitious interest in a shiksa's flesh, or allow one to have a pinch more than another. They kept a wary eye on each other, but it was still dodgems for me when they were about. With Lew it was impossible. He was only eighteen years old but already engaged to a very sweet pretty girl. She lived far out in the suburbs – they could only meet twice a week and his masculinity was on the boil all the time. He tried to assuage it a little by kissing me at every possible opportunity. When he caught me with my hands full it was difficult to dodge him so that he didn't get my lips. It was impossible to feel mad at him – he was like an oversexed puppy full of joy and daring. He would come into the scullery on pretext of sniffing appreciatively over what Momma was stirring on the gas stove and take a quick nip at the back of my neck. It made me a bag of nerves even if it did add a spice of flavour to the day. He was always on the razor's edge of discovery – his very daring made me laugh, quite undoing the value of the terrible scowls I gave him to warn him off.

Father's words, 'We know thee'lt be a good little wench and not do anything to let thee old Mam and Dad down', was a very effective chastity belt for locking out temptation. It was lucky Lew's father didn't know about his attentions. 'Poppa' was a highly orthodox little Jew. The bronchial asthma which racked him made him small and thin, and I sometimes wondered where he had room to keep all the terrible coughs which sent him into purple-faced paroxysms. Sometimes there was only me about when the old gentleman was taken by a spasm so cruel it seemed determined to choke him there and then. In a dilemma of pity I did not know whether to offend the dignity of the man by putting my arms round his shoulders to steady him – being only a shiksa and a maid at that – or whether to stand helpless and endure the watching. I often did the former – he gave no sign of feeling offence. Every January and February when the London fog was at its worst, his elder sons paid for him to stay in a nursing home in Bognor.

Fifteen-year-old Moishe rejoiced in this escape from the Talmud. Every evening, black cap on head, he was made to study it for a long period. When his father left the room for a coughing session Moishe read the comic folded between the pages. Not being religious myself, I didn't blame him – what with his school homework he didn't have much time for recreation – as long as the old gentleman thought Moishe was religious that was all that mattered. I had a very soft spot for handsome Moishe – didn't he put on the records I liked over and over again on the old wind-up gramophone whenever he could? What could be better than Richard Tauber singing *You Are My Heart's Delight*, to gild the spirits of a seventeen-year-old romantic?

Blessed with little initiative of my own, I stayed with the Cohens over two years without thought of getting another job, or of asking for a rise – they hadn't thought of that either.

However a girl from our village had found a job in a young lady students' college hall near Tottenham Court Road – she wrote to me recommending I get one there too. A vacancy for a kitchen-maid was coming up, the wages were twelve-and-six a week, the food excellent and plentiful, half a day off a week – and a whole day every third Sunday. The only snag was that I'd have to wear servant's uniform – which meant spending my bit of savings on the hated stuff and forgoing a visit back home before starting there.

Mrs Cohen offered me fifteen shillings a week to stay on. However the old restlessness had started to work again, and whatever pangs I might feel about leaving this household – especially dear Becky – I knew that as long as I was in service I could never be more than a migrant worker at someone else's table.

# College Hall

After my own home, I had found the Cohens' kitchen hugely spacious; but the kitchen at College Hall was like looking through a magnifying-glass. The whole ground floor of the Aldgate house would have fitted into one corner of it. No expense had been spared to equip it with steamer trays, cooking stoves, and a hot-plate big enough to hide Ali Baba and his forty thieves. There were sinks for this and sinks for that, some big enough to have a bath in. The only thing the planners left out was a pair of roller-skates to cut out the walking.

As well as the kitchen proper, an enormous scullery, a walk-in larder, a servery, a servant's hall, brush cupboards, staff cloak-rooms, and the grandly large student's dining-room occupied the semi-basement floor. There were twenty living-in maids, four daily women, and two cooks; not your ordinary cooks, these were lady-cooks, who ate in their own private quarters, spoke with upper-crust accents, and had *Cordon Bleu* qualifications.

In charge of all the domestic arrangements was Miss Delaine, so grand and remote in her office we hardly ever saw her; then nice, kindly, middle-aged Miss Robson, the bursar, and genteel Miss Mander, the secretary, engager of staff. I suppose Dorcas, the telephonist and receptionist was next in the hierarchy, but it was difficult to know where to place her. She fetched her meals from the servants' hall on a tray, and ate in the privacy of her cosy little room by the front door. She wore a bottle-green uniform, with cream cap and apron, while we kitchen-maids wore blue print dresses, and the house-maids and parlour-maids black. Dorcas looked down her nose at the rest of us, and she was a tale-bearer to Miss Mander of every little misdemeanour, or short cuts to the housework, she could discover. She was thoroughly disliked by all the domestic staff. There were about eighty lady-students, mostly upper middle-class by birth.

The place was a sea of bums and bosoms, a vast hen-house with no resident cockerel. If something remotely personable in trousers came through the doors, it was he who had to do the dodging! We three kitchen-maids were even grateful for the sour masculine grunt the sole man about the place, old Spackman, gave us. Spackman arrived only to disappear again to stoke and feed the incinerator and boilers at the end of a labyrinth of underground passages.

I doubt if 'old' Spackman was more than fifty. His calling seemed to have dried up his tongue, and given a patina of ashy greyness to his hair, skin, clothes, and outlook. He seemed safe enough in this female jungle.

Though the students had a centrally heated, carpeted bedroom each, with a bathroom between three, we maids did not do so badly. True, we were three to a room, and only had mats by our beds and no central heating, but being highest up we had the most panoramic views of the roofs, and we had two bathrooms between us, with hot pipes to dry our stockings and smalls.

Being able to have a bath nearly every day was a novel luxury I wallowed in, literally. At the Cohens', the whole family, as well as I, had to troop down to the public baths once a week, and get back before it was time to light the Shabbes candles.

This was the first job in which I had official and recognised time off. My half-day rarely coincided with that of the girl who had got me the job. No matter, I was very happy to slip off to the pictures, and change identities with the woman star of the film.

Knowing I was considered plain as a child, the idea had stuck, and as a rule I gave practically no thought to my appearance. I was still under the illusion that men fell in love with a pretty face, and I never assumed that my figure would hold any attraction for them. Yet I had a tiny waist, and a long period of good food and plenty of work had developed me nicely in all the right places.

My fellow-workers used to scold me for my lack of interest, so to placate them one half-day off, I decided to dress myself up. I had washed my hair, and I let one of them put it in curlers. After my bath, I decided to put on a dress bought a long time ago at a jumble sale. It was in navy lock-knit wool with pale blue striped trimming in the yoke. I had to tug and pull at it a bit until I had smoothed it over me as closely fitting as a second skin.

A bit tight, I thought, but never mind, it was not far to walk to the Dominion, Tottenham Court Road, where a film starring Clark Gable was showing. I combed out my hair, now a silky cascade of wavy curls to my shoulders, and finished my ensemble with a navy-blue beret perched, as was the fashion, on one side of my head. Neither of my room-mates was there to approve the transformation. Only one of the cooks was in the kitchen, and she opened her mouth in considerable astonishment as I walked through the door. She looked as though she were going to say something, but must have recollected she was a lady and just stared at me instead.

Along Tottenham Court Road a lot of other people, especially men, seemed to be pointedly staring at me too. A pair of them, in the City gear of bowler hats, dark suits and gold-headed canes, stopped in their tracks, raised their hats, gave little simultaneous bows, and smiling in the most complimentary manner, said something in a language I thought was Latin.

I was not quite sure if this pantomime was for my benefit at first but then a bus passed, and a young man holding on to the rail at the bottom of the stairs, called out to me to 'wait for him'. He was a perfect stranger!

There was so much head-turning in my direction, I got quite worried that something was amiss. Oh, there was Kath, my room-mate. 'Hey, Kath, is there anything wrong with me at the back? People seem to be staring at me, I wondered if something was showing.'

'I should think something *is* showing, practically everything you've got! It's that dress, it's a mile too tight.'

I decided to go back to College Hall and change. I was waylaid by a street photographer already developing the picture he had taken of me. It cost me sixpence. I looked at it, and thought all I needed was two French blokes and we could have gone straight into one of those apache dances.

Kath came back shortly after me, and drew some of the other maids' attention to my plight. One of the more sophisticated ones took my measurements, 37"–20"–39", and in that frock! 'Crikey, no wonder some of their eyes was poppin' out!'

I had a new awareness; I was a little richer than I had thought, but almost clueless how to spend my wares. Also after seeing the film I was only interested in someone like Clark Gable.

Life was very comfortable in my College Hall job. My only pangs came when I scraped out all the custard, milk pudding and gravies, that were left in the cooking utensils after dishing-up. If only, by some magic means, I could send them home! I bought wool, and knitted vests and jumpers for my little sisters, and sent Mam an occasional postal order, little enough, yet I was always broke the last week of the month.

When my Sunday off came around I did not care if I were broke. London was outside the door, I had long strong young legs, and like Felix I could keep on walking. Freedom to go out was still precious enough to be exciting.

I was going to say I followed my nose, but that would have taken me skywards. I just put one foot in front of the other, and everywhere was fascinating. People, and shop-windows to gaze at; the quiet of the City, still with cobbled side streets, and dark little shops with bottle-glass windows.

Sometimes my Sunday-off meanderings took me through some of London's magic names, Fleet Street, Lincoln's Inn, Cheapside and Shaftesbury Avenue, where the pictures of the actors and actresses appearing in the theatres were displayed outside. They actually appeared here *in the flesh*! Names like Jack Buchanan, Elsie Randolph, Margaretta Scott, Isobel Elsom, Gladys Cooper, Fay Compton, Nigel Playfair; names that had a fairy-tale remoteness about them, when I had seen their photographs on bits of paper torn from newspapers and periodicals and hung up in our privy back home.

How lucky was I, Polly Mason from the Forest of Dean, to be able to tread these hallowed streets.

I had no money to buy food, but the physical hunger never got sharp enough to make me turn round until a clock somewhere reminded me I *must* be in by ten o'clock. It was no problem finding my way; I would ask some kindly-looking woman, she would tell me what bus to catch, and I just walked the bus routes back to Tottenham Court Road. I knew my fellow kitchen-maids would have left me more than enough supper in the hot plate to make up for my missed meals.

I had no one to share the emotions my secret love inspired. I tried desperately to write it all down. When I left College Hall, I consigned a pile of scribbled efforts to the incinerator.

The young lady residents were allowed to go on the roof of College Hall, a privilege which was barred to us domestics. To reach the roof the students had to pass the end of the corridor where the maids' bedrooms were. One day I was just coming out on to our back stairs, when a student came down from the roof. She was a Canadian, and apparently not very familiar with the then rigid English class system. She started to talk to me. Our conversation became so animated she followed me down our staircase until she came to the floor where her bedroom was. We were still talking and laughing when Miss Mander came by. Her smile for the student was pretty chilly, but the look she gave me was a real freezer.

The next day I was summoned to Miss Robson's office for a

lecture in proper decorum for kitchen-maids, which most certainly did not include their talking in a familiar manner with any of the students.

Having choked on this bitter pill nearly all night and not being able to swallow it, next morning I asked to be allowed to speak to Miss Robson. Hurt pride had puffed me up on to my very high horse, which has no bridle, alas, and now I was ready to give *her* a lecture, and my month's notice to go with it.

That morning I did not go into prayers, which were attended by everyone resident in the main hall. That omission alone would have got me summoned to Miss Robson's presence.

At ten o'clock I was told by one of the lady cooks that Miss Robson would see me, but first I must put on a clean apron and cap.

'Come in,' called Miss Robson, and I stood squarely in front of her, my head held a bit on the high side. She asked me why had I not attended prayers that morning, and reminded me once again that I had been seen talking and laughing on the stairs with one of the lady students.

Now, yet more incensed than in the first interview, I told her that she had got it a little bit wrong. The young lady had got into conversation with *me*. Secondly, if I was not fit to talk to the students, how could I talk to God, who I was under the impression was considered a good deal superior to any student.

'You do not talk to God. You pray to God, and pray that He may listen to you,' Miss Robson reprimanded me, but her tone was not unkind.

'Well, even if I'm praying to Him, if we're all good enough to do that together in His presence, why aren't we good enough to talk to each other?'

Miss Robson gave a deep sigh, and then a kindly-meant lecture on humility. She herself would have to curtsey to royalty, we all had our place in society, and ducks could never be happy trying to pretend they were swans. Far better for me if I knew my place and made the best of it.

I agreed with her that College Hall was a very good place for the servants, but she could now offer mine to a more deserving girl, as I was giving my notice in there and then.

It is a credit to this good lady that she tried to persuade me to alter my mind. I very firmly refused her kind offer. After my previous jobs I thought perhaps I had cut off my nose to spite my face, but I felt a kind of glory in my rebellion. I sang *The Red Flag* as loud as I dared among the clatter of the pots and pans, and thought of my Dad and all the downtrodden workers in the world, and nearly cried.

On my next half-day off I went to look for another job. One of the maids told me about a domestic servant agency in the Edgware Road. The lady who ran it gave me three jobs to apply for, the third one with some apparent reluctance. 'I don't think it is really your sort of job,' she mused. It was for a domestic help in a bed-and-breakfast hotel in a terrace not far from Paddington station. It was the nearest on her list, so disregarding her comment I thought I would apply there first.

The terrace ran from Edgware Road to Lancaster Gate. The tall houses looked elegant on each side fronted by a row of trees in a narrow, grassy, iron-railed enclosure. I hoped at once I would get the job; the trees were an unexpected bounty.

The number I wanted was a corner house, another good omen, for it added to the illusion of space. There was a short flight of steps up to the front door, and a longer flight of steps down to the area and the back door.

Oh well, I was not a servant there yet. Still smarting from my 'telling-off' at College Hall, and in militant mood, I rang the front door bell.

# The Boarding-House

I had the physical advantage of looking down on the lady of the boarding-house, for it was she, a Miss Lowry, who answered the bell.

Frizzy, light sandy hair topped a pale, flaccid face; even the freckles on it looked anaemic. Her short neck seemed to have run into her bosom, which in turn appeared to have run into her flabby belly. An unbaked dough sort of person.

She had a very friendly manner, which did not alter when I told her I was after the job as maid, and not applying for a room.

No, the post had not been filled; the wages were fifteen shillings a week. Time off, from three p.m. to seven p.m. on every alternate day; off duty from seven p.m. the other days.

Seven p.m. till when?

That would be entirely up to me; I would have my own key to the front door.

Uniform?

No, as long as I looked smart and clean in an overall.

She gave me all this information standing in the small hall inside the front door. My own key of the door! My own key of the *front* door! I was just coming up to twenty-one, and now I really felt like it! No hated caps and aprons! Fifteen shillings a week, and all that time off! A tree outside, as well! And that lady in the domestic agency saying she didn't think it was my sort of job! I felt sick with apprehension lest I did not get it.

'You would share a room downstairs with the other maid; she's older than you, a funny sort in some ways, but I think you would get on with her all right. Would you like to see the room?'

The room was small and drab, in a drab basement, next to a drab kitchen. One other small basement room was let to a permanent boarder, and Miss Lowry herself had the big one.

When she opened the door at the narrow end of the hall leading to the basement, the concentration of hot ashy fumes from a coke boiler nearly made me choke.

I did not care if the room had been as black as a dungeon, and the air like fog; it was a small price to pay for the privilege of using the same door as everyone else.

Did I think the job would suit me? I felt the question should have been would I suit the job? She appeared to have taken me on there and then. I gave her Miss Robson's name and address for a reference and explained I must work out my notice. However, if I heard no further from Miss Lowry within a week, the job was mine.

Two weeks went by, I heard nothing, the job was mine. Lucky, lucky me!

One more week to go. It was the morning of my twenty-first birthday, a fact I had barely taken note of. There had never been any spare money for celebrating birthdays, even with a card, in my childhood; so birthdays have never been important to me. When I was summoned to Miss Robson's office, my heart sank. Perhaps Miss Lowry had been slow in writing for a reference, and now Miss Robson was going to say she could not give me one?

But, no. There was Miss Robson giving me a friendly smile and handing me a little parcel for my birthday. I was so surprised, I did not know how to thank her properly, before she asked me if I had found another job.

I told her I had, and where it was, and that I would have a key of my own, and lots of free time. I did not mean to be unpleasant, I just wanted her to know how lucky I was. Surprisingly, she shook her greying head sadly.

'Well, Winifred, I don't care for the sound of this job; they haven't applied to me for a reference, which is not a good sign. Now I want you to think it over carefully. I've engaged a replacement for you, but that doesn't matter; you may still stay on until you find a more suitable situation.'

The bad name of the Paddington area obviously meant something to Miss Robson, but I had no idea why she should take this attitude. Because of this my thanks were somewhat insincere.

My parcel from Miss Robson contained scented writing-paper and envelopes. When I expressed surprise to the other two kitchen-maids, their surprise was even greater that I had not mentioned my birthday, and the twenty-first at that! Hadn't my family sent me a card? Oh, what a shame!

By teatime my misfortune had spread through to the other girls, and I was being made much fuss of. I wrote home post-haste, sending the money for Mam to send me a birthday card to shut them up. And so she did, by return, a grand one, with a big gold key on the front. I was thrilled and pleased to receive it.

Lest you think me entirely ungracious – when a few weeks later the domestic staff at College Hall went down like ninepins to a scourge of 'flu, I went round there for over a month and spent all my spare time working like a Trojan wherever I could best be put to use.

When all the staff had recuperated, Miss Robson, herself ill with 'flu, sent me a written message that there would always be a job for me at College Hall as long as she was in residence.

My helpful attitude brought me the reward again of the excellent College Hall food, an item that was lamentably short at the Terrace; and I was able to take some of it back to Joan, the other maid.

Miss Lowry shared her room with an enormous neutered tom cat which she adored. Most mornings she would send me up to Ginger's, a butcher in Edgware Road for three penn'orth of cat's meat. The best of these pieces she kept for the cat, and the rest, with a penn'orth of pot-herbs, made the stew for our dinner. For breakfast we had the same as the boarders, a piece of thinly cut streaky bacon, and a fried egg. We also had toast, and any of the marmalade left on the boarders' trays. After dinner we sometimes had a swiss bun, then three for two pence, as a sweet, or maybe, one of Miss Lowry's rice puddings.

The rice puddings of College Hall would not have owned one of hers even as a poor relation. College puddings were made with a cupful of rice, two cupfuls of sugar, and two quarts of top-grade milk, steamed for eight hours until milk and rice had changed into a thick pinky-yellow cream with a rich golden skin on top.

Miss Lowry used a cupful of cheap rice, a couple of spoons of sugar, a pint of water with a dash of milk, and she cooked it until the rice grains had swollen enough to make a nodding acquaintance with each other.

The rest of the day we had to subsist on tea and toast, and go easy on the bread for that. About that time a sweet named Mars Bars came out, and most days Joan and I kept going on one each. Miss Lowry had her own cache of goodies in her room.

After Joan and I had taken the eighteen trays round on my first morning, you could have knocked me down with a feather duster when she said, 'Come on, cocky, we'll go back to our bedroom,' where we sat down on our beds. From under hers she took a wind-up gramophone and played several times over her repertoire of three records – *Laugh, clown laugh, Charmaine,* and *My Diane.*

After the brisk efficiency of College Hall, I got into quite a sweat waiting for Miss Lowry to come and tell us off.

'Don't you drop yer drawers frettin' about *'er*,' Joan sniffed, puffing away at the first Woodbine of the day.

I had not cottoned on then that Joan had some kind of hold over Miss Lowry. I never did find out quite what it was, but it was something to do with a man. Had Miss Lowry's highly religious father found out about it, it would probably have brought on the threatened heart attack. Mr Lowry was not supposed to know the reason why his daughter could charge such high prices for bed and breakfast. Nor, at that time, did I realise why Miss Robson had been so opposed to my new job.

Sometimes it was difficult for me to know whether Joan or Miss Lowry was my boss. It was a delicate situation for Miss Lowry. Joan being rather lazy, the only way Miss Lowry could get Joan's part of the staircase paint washed down was to threaten her with the sack. Although Joan made dark hints about letting out secrets, she seemed to prefer to flounce up the stairs with a bucket of hot water into every stair-tread corner, rather than pack her case, get Miss Lowry into hot water, and clear out. Nevertheless the little mystery remained.

I stayed at that Paddington boarding-house for eighteen months, and my eyes were opened to life styles and personalities which would have been completely alien to anyone living in our village. For boarding-houses come second only to asylums in collecting a rich and varied population of human eccentrics.

Of the eighteen rooms for letting, eight were occupied by 'permanents'. The cheap top-floor rooms mostly served as nest-boxes for eggheads – students of one kind or another. Judging by the bags under their eyes and the fact that they were permanently broke, they were also studying the more gaudy aspects of London's night life. When we had the 'Room to Let' notice over the door, it was always like a little adventure to answer the bell. There was a constant stream of overnight visitors for the rooms – couples, usually, with anonymous names and faces, and little or no luggage.

Many of the permanents I still remember vividly today. A maid, like a barber or hairdresser, makes good blotting paper for the outpouring of human feelings. Absorbing snippets of autobiographical confession came my way, from the lonely, the unhappy, the angry, and the kindly who had no family of their own.

Miss Player and Miss Wills, who occupied ground-floor rooms, were night-club hostesses. One was beautiful, the archetypal dumb blonde, thick as a brick and the ideal cure for any tired business man. Her beauty and youth gave her the security of ten pounds a week as the mistress of a wealthy man. The other, Miss Wills, was a sad example of what many Miss Players grow into. She was fat, common, aimless and suicidally unhappy. The days of being kept were long over for Miss Wills, and she only remained in her job because Miss Player would have left too if the management sacked her. The Miss Players of this world are a club-owner's dream.

Then there was Miss O'Rory, who had a room on the first floor. She suffered from bronchial asthma and was arthritic as well. Despite her poor health, she never missed her daily walk. Winter and summer she wore an ancient Harris tweed coat and battered brown felt hat, yet no one could ever have mistaken her for a member of the lower classes. She was one of the eight children of an Irish rector, and having been a rebel had become separated from her family. She bragged that for many years she had lived in the South of France as the mistress of a famous artist. Yet, when the Jubilee of George V took place, she insisted that I, who should have been on duty, place a chair by the front door for her so that I could pop up to the Edgware Road to see the procession. Old and broken-winded Miss O'Rory might have been, but she was a thoroughbred.

Mr Davis, who had a big room on the same floor, was something in the city. He looked the part too when he left each morning for the stock exchange complete with bowler hat, brief-case, spats and umbrella. As he went away at weekends and was one of Joan's 'breakfasts' I saw very little of him, and wasn't much bothered about that.

It was quite different when Mr O'Brien arrived.

'Ooh, isn't he *lovely*!' I enthused to Joan after I had taken in his breakfast.

There he was asleep with his crinkly dark wavy hair against the white pillow, his long dark lashes and pinky-bronzed face contrasting so nicely with his silky blue pyjamas. He looked even better when he opened his blue eyes and smiled at me. His room smelled sweetly of scented soap, and a single rose in a glass by his bedside table just completed the picture.

He looked like a film star, and I told Joan so. She gave one of her sniffs – she was always giving one of her sniffs about somebody, and said: 'Well, what d'you expect, 'im being one o' them?'

One of them? What did she mean by that, and sounding so contemptuous? Perhaps it was because he was an actor.

I didn't ask Joan to enlarge on her comments then, but I found out what she meant one morning when I took up Mr O'Brien's breakfast. Another male head was poking out of the bedclothes beside his.

'Bring up another breakfast tray, please,' said Mr O'Brien.

Bring up another! Indeed, he shouldn't have one. I marched downstairs, plonked down the tray, and told Miss Lowry I wasn't going to wait on the likes of him. I did not properly know what 'the likes of him' meant, but if inexperience and intolerance are the parents of judgement, I had plenty of both.

Poor Mr O'Brien, he had to go.

Eventually Mr Davis left to marry a middle-aged woman of Amazonian proportions (she could easily have carried him off under her arm!) and his place was taken by Angela Mandcope. Her arrival in London was given a line or two in the gossip columns of the evening papers, for she was a well-known artist from South Africa. Her nephew, a former student resident, had recommended the place. Angela Mandcope was divorced, about forty, small, dark, attractive-looking, restless and chatty.

She was very friendly to us, but somehow I couldn't take to her. Every day she was visited by a very upper-crust young man who was quite good-looking in a thin, fair sort of way. His name was Neville.

She had her hooks well and truly into him, having met him on his uncle's estate in South Africa. Mrs Mandcope asked if I would like to pose for her sometimes in my free time, in the nude of course, and I wouldn't mind Neville wandering in and out, would I?

By now, I was getting used to eccentrics and their odd ideas, so I declined quite politely. But her next offer left me temporarily speechless, despite the fact that I always was and always will be a 'chopsy mouth'.

Neville, she told me, was the only son of a lord, she and he were passionately in love and wanted to get married. There was no hope because this noble lord demanded that his son should marry someone who could produce male heirs for the family fortune and name. Mrs Mandcope could have no children.

Now, if Neville could present to his father a bonny healthy son he could prove was his, whom they could then adopt, Neville reckoned that his father would assent to the marriage. Neville agreed with her that I would do very nicely to bear his baby. Of course, when I could no longer work I should be comfortably kept, have the baby in a good nursing home, and be paid a lump sum of at least a hundred pounds. If it should be a girl, I could keep the baby if I wished.

I was so shocked and hurt by this proposition, I could not answer her. I walked down to the basement wounded to the heart.

I felt defiled through no fault of my own. How often, to myself, had I pictured myself married. My husband would be someone kind and wise like my father, whose grey eyes would have crinkly corners, who would have the manners and presence of Clark Gable. There would be a house with pretty curtains and cushions, and nice lace-edged cloths for the table. Then one day there would be my own babies, precious bundles to love and dress up and dote upon. A dream of future love, tied up for the present in the ribbons of hope. Now these romantic notions had been raped by suggestions so cold, so heartless, so insulting, I was hurt beyond measure.

That the conception of a child could be arranged like a business deal, and that that child, one's own flesh and blood, be handed over to someone else for money! The icy shock brought on a mood of cold fury. Master Neville had better not come near me! After a few days my mood softened. Perhaps he knew nothing about it. She was a lunatic, and desperate to make a good matrimonial catch; such people should not be judged seriously.

I was on duty one evening, cleaning and filling up the cruets at the kitchen table, when Neville himself came down to the kitchen. He had the air and ingratiating manner of a man about to ask a favour.

Let it be for a pot of tea and toast for two! Please God, don't let him repeat her monstrous suggestion to me! But, after some humming and hawing, and admittedly with some diffidence, he broached the subject.

Cruel in my scorn, I told him that I would have smacked his face but that I had more respect for my hand. That even if his father were a lord and he fancied himself a member of the privileged classes, it did not give him the right to consider I was as debased as himself and Mrs Mandcope. What's more, for his information, people who did menial tasks and were forced to wait on their inferiors had warm blood in their veins, and deep feelings, and were, 'inconsiderately, perhaps', part of the same human race of which he thought himself so superior a member . . . etc., etc.

He went upstairs in a very different mood from the one he came down in. He was pale-faced, ruffled and shamed, but I had no pity for him and certainly none for her. I was thankful that Mrs Mandcope left the boarding-house almost at once.

I was soon to learn that infatuation can make fools and villains of us all, and that my judgement might have been more tempered.

'Number seventeen,' Joan told me one evening. 'Mr Gordon's back. You'll like him, he used to have number twelve until he went to Canada. He's been gone a year; but now he's back to get a degree. Not a hap'orth of trouble, and a proper gentleman.' High praise indeed, from Joan! I was glad he was one of my 'breakfasts'. I looked forward to seeing this paragon.

At seven-thirty sharp I knocked at number seventeen. A deep, male voice answered sleepily, 'Come in.' I saw his forehead and cow's lick of dark hair first; then his whole face emerged from the blankets.

My dream man! Kind, grey eyes with crinkly corners, well-marked but not too bushy eyebrows, a straight firm nose, and a mouth full enough for tenderness, but firm enough for a strong character. A nicely balanced mixture of Clark Gable and my Dad!

A pipe and tobacco pouch lay on the bedside table, a tweed sports jacket and haversack hung behind the door. A real masculine aura. His voice had a Clark Gable drawl as well, and his smile was even more knee-weakening as he sat up and said: 'Good morning, ma-am.'

I floated all the way downstairs. It must be Fate, to bring a man looking like my ideal lover to this very place. Joan had given me a start in the build-up; now I had seen the façade, and I proceeded to stuff Mr Gordon with every virtue known to the male sex. I worshipped him. Had he said to me, 'Winnie, I fancy you should get on the roof and chuck yourself off this morning,' I would have willingly done it to please him.

If he was aware of my adulation, he did not show it. He did not have to; a few words from him went round in my mind like a record with the needle stuck in a groove until he spoke to me again. Each room had a numbered box in the hall which the tenants could change to 'in' or 'out'. I was sad when his box said 'out', and a love-lorn droop when it said 'in'.

He slept three floors above my basement room, but was as remote and desirable as a Hollywood film star. I had put him on a pedestal, a god of my own making, so that I might have the exquisite torture of being hopelessly in love. It kept me easily immune from the skirmishing attacks on my virtue that were inevitable in a setting like a Paddington terrace boarding-house.

To have Mr Gordon in number seventeen redressed the balance for all the wicked men in the world. It didn't occur to me to question what he was doing about sex. He never brought any girls home. I imagined he was living in a state of pure celibacy until Miss Right should come along.

Then Joan dropped a bombshell – she quietly gave in a week's notice. I already knew that Joan was a woman of means. She had been awarded £400 many years ago, as a result of an injury. She had saved up a nest-egg from her wages to go with it, and was going into partnership in a shop, with her married sister. She was very thrilled about this venture, and as a bonus washed the whole of the staircase paintwork from top to bottom before she left.

From the same domestic agency that I had come from Miss Lowry got a replacement maid; a girl named Rosie, and anyone less like a rose would be hard to visualise. One could picture her a thin grey little rodent climbing out of the Paddington Canal and nearly turning into a girl. Had she filled her narrow lungs with a good gust of fresh air the shock might have been disastrous. 'Narrow' is the word that comes to mind to describe Rosie physically. She had a long thin pallid face, well sprinkled with pimples and blackheads; her nose was long and just kept her small grey eyes apart. She looked as sly as a ferret.

Narrow, physically, she may have been; but her mind and her morals were as broad as her horizons stretched. She was engagingly frank, even to her own disadvantage.

She was engaged to a baker's roundsman, and as willing to pop into bed with him as with any other man who gave her the chance. Sex to her was like fish and chips, enjoyable, but nothing to make a fuss about. In the male-female spectrum I would have placed her and Mr Gordon at opposite extremes.

She had been at the boarding-house about a fortnight, when Mr Gordon was about to go up to his Lancashire home for the long summer vacation. Instead of going out on her evening off she must have gone upstairs. She came down about an hour later to get ready to meet her regular boy-friend. As she changed, she gave me a running commentary on Mr Gordon's sexual powers and habits in bed. At first, her words would not, could not, sink in. I looked at her ugly little face, skinny straight figure, and her general air of having knocked about an awful lot.

Was Mr Gordon, that god among men, so bereft of female companionship that he must have the likes of *her*? His modesty seemed fantastic; he was worthy of the most beautiful woman in the world! *I* was a few notches better all round than Rosie; he could have *me*; oh, if only I knew how to go about this business of sex!

So disheartened was I, that I almost finished with men before I started with them. Yet his face, with his crinkly-cornered eyes, his nose, his mouth, his pipe-smoking tweedy air, the way his hair grew in a cow's-lick from his forehead, was to haunt my memory for many years.

# A Job for Life

Between going to the pictures, and happenings in the boarding-house, my life did not lack its little dramas. But I gradually became aware of something sinister and unwholesome happening in the streets of London. Sometimes I saw bands of black-shirted youths marching about led by a politician named Mosley.

Their choice of black for a uniform seemed evil in itself. Most of them wore jackboots and marched like the German Nazi soldiers I had seen in the newsreels. They seemed full of anger and hate and were looking for something to vent it on.

Why were they allowed to darken our streets? What did they want? 'They're taking a leaf out of that Hitler's book; they want to destroy the Jews,' some said. But why?

What had the Jews done to them? I thought of my life in the Jewish household at Aldgate. There they were, working like beavers, wishing no harm or unkindness to anyone. If I had to choose whom to live among, I would run back to Aldgate quick rather than mix with the sort represented by that black-shirted lot of bullies.

I was put more in the political picture one evening when a group of young people came to the front door. Their spokesman was Sheila Lynd, daughter of the writer Robert Lynd, and the group were distributing anti-Mosley leaflets. She stayed half an hour, explaining his devious methods of trying to get political power. She asked me if I would join an anti-Mosley rally in the East End the following Sunday.

It would be my half-day off and I was in just the mood to vent my anger on someone. That Mosley and his black-shirted crew would do nicely. Let any one of them dare lay a finger on a hair of my Becky's head!

Yes, I would join a young Communist group going down to the East End to stop the Mosley march through there. Among the group with Sheila Lynd was a good-looking fellow who promised to call for me.

By now, with Joan's departure and my infatuation with Mr Gordon turning into a sad memory, I had had enough of the boarding-house. I was fed up; I was ready for a change, ready for some adventure. I gave Miss Lowry two weeks' notice. I had decided to find digs or a room for myself and take a job as a waitress.

Sure enough, on the Sunday afternoon, the young man called for me with a few more anti-Mosleyites. We got on the underground at Praed Street.

When the train stopped at Edgware Road, a much larger contingent got in. A young man among this group seemed to have taken it upon himself to act as spokesman. He waved his arms about and spoke rather loudly, and in my mean fashion I mentally labelled him a 'bighead'. He was accompanied by a beautiful, quiet sort of girl, whom I took to be his girl-friend.

'Fancy,' I thought, 'a nice ladylike girl, and so good-looking too, going out with a show-off like him!'

He was quite a handsome young man, and when I momentarily caught the look he gave me I did note that he had nice, big, soft brown eyes.

'Hiya, Greening,' he addressed my companion.

'Hiya, Syd.'

'That's Syd Foley and his sister,' my escort informed me; not that I was interested.

Before I lost my escort in the mêlée of crowds and foot and mounted police at Aldgate, he had told me a political meeting was being held the following Thursday over a pub in the Shirland Road, Maida Vale. I was off duty that evening and I was keen to go.

Mixing with this group of young left-wing idealists gave me something else to think about, and helped take my mind off Mr Gordon. Some of them belonged to the Labour League of Youth, some to the Young Communists League, some to the Peace Pledge Union, and some to all three!

They certainly had a love-hate relationship with society. They loved the exploited, and hated the exploiters and aggressors. They all seemed to seek goodness, but were hot-headed and blinkered up to the eyebrows with political prejudices.

On Thursday I was among the first comers and took a seat at the end of the front row of chairs. Quite a small crowd turned up – the last of the stragglers was that talkative Syd Foley off the train. Before he took a seat at the back, his glance seemed to sweep casually over the attendance.

I had absorbed quite a bit of political groundwork as I sat on the corner of the fender at home listening to Dad arguing and discussing with his butties. On politics at least I was inclined to question statements before swallowing them whole.

One speaker exhorted us to shop at the Co-op where profits were redistributed as dividends to the customers. I had tasted Co-op cocoa! What, I demanded to know, were the salaries of the highly paid Co-op officials? They seemed to me to be in the capitalist managing director's bracket. Down with such salaries, and higher dividends instead, was my resolution. No wonder the Co-op prices couldn't compete with Lewis's cut-price shop in Church Street. Whilst I was at it, I had a go at high-salaried socialist politicians – they were capitalists too, selling ideals wrapped up with the gift of the gab. They contributed nothing materially to society, but liked to enjoy the high standard of living of the 'enemy'.

A university graduate dealt with my points – he wrapped up the answers in so much verbose intellectual flannel that I was all at sea and wished I'd kept my mouth shut.

During the meeting I had exchanged a few words with a nice cockney girl sitting next to me, and when it was over we walked down the stairs together. I noticed Syd Foley joined us – he and the girl appeared to know each other.

Compared with his behaviour in the train, he kept very quiet, leaving the chatting to us as we walked up Warwick Avenue to the Edgware Road. Here I had to turn right for my walk back to the Terrace, and my companion left for Kilburn. I bid them both good night, having taken it for granted that Syd was escorting the other girl home. To my surprise he too wished her good night and asked if he might walk on with me. I told him where I worked and said if it wasn't taking him out of his way I had no objection. Oh, it was on his way, he said (the fibber).

We talked politics right to the door. I did fumble a bit unnecessarily in my bag to find my key, but he just said good night without a hint of wishing to see me again. I was a bit piqued, but not much bothered.

The next morning on the mat inside the hall was a hand-delivered note addressed to me. Would I perhaps consider going to the pictures with him? He had found out the telephone number of the boarding-house, and would ring for my answer that evening. We arranged to go to the pictures on Saturday. I asked him to come at half past six.

When I was sent to the butcher's on Saturday morning for the cat's meat, I made a few purchases of my own – a thick lamb chop, half a pound of sausages, a gammon rasher and some bread rolls. I had noticed when we walked down the Edgware Road that when the wind blew against Syd's mac he looked as thin as an exclamation mark!

Miss Lowry always spent Saturday night at her father's home in Neasden. Rosie hung around the kitchen with her mouth drooling while I cooked Syd's meal. I plonked a sausage between a bread roll and told her to make herself scarce. After Mr Gordon I couldn't afford to have her hanging about.

Syd was prompt in arriving, and showed a gratifying appreciation for the unexpected meal – the lot went down. I excused myself and went into the bedroom so he could pick up his chop for the last juicy fragments instead of trying to worry them off with a knife and fork. I had noticed that the cuffs of his jacket were on the verge of fraying – he was obviously not a young man of means.

I dabbed on some extra perfume – June Night was the name. Rosie kindly offered to wash up.

'I thought you would like to see the film at the "Select",' said Syd as we approached the Edgware Road. The 'Select' was a tiny cinema known locally by two other names, 'The Flea Pit' and 'The Hole in the Wall'. Seats were sixpence, a shilling, and one-and-six. I didn't need to be clairvoyant to know where we would be sitting. I thought of his coat cuffs. I'd like to pay for myself, I said, putting my sixpence down for the cashier. There was no embarrassed argument from Syd. Contrariwise I thought: mean bugger, he'd better watch out if he's one of the wandering hand brigade.

We had been sitting inside for a long time before he shyly put an arm round my shoulder and drew my head near to his. This was nice – I felt protected and very content. When the lights went up for the ice-cream sellers he reached into his pocket and brought out two apples – the sort the barrow boys flogged at knock-down prices, small, wizened, but still sound enough to eat. We both managed to appear very uninterested in ice-cream, and settled back down until 'God save the King'. Syd didn't kiss me, he didn't even ask for one on the doorstep. All the same, he asked for another date a few evenings hence. By then I hoped to have found some digs.

I found my digs on the top floor of a slummy house in Molyneux Street which ran parallel with the Edgware Road. It was smelly and dark – some of the tenants lit a candle at night and put it on a shelf on the landing, but there were still plenty of dark corners for the bugs to take a walk. My room was the smaller of two rented by an Irishwoman for eleven shillings. She charged me eight shillings for mine. 'Mrs' Flaherty was fat, fair and fortyish – and she certainly had a weakness for 'a dhrap o' the hard stuff'. She shared the room with her little daughter Annie, then six years old. 'Mrs' was a courtesy title only – she had never married.

For my eight shillings rent she reckoned to include a pint of paraffin each week for the little oil lamp and small iron contraption I could cook on. They both gave off more smoke than an Indian on the warpath. Instead, I bought candles, and an occasional seven-pound bag of coal to light a fire in the tiny grate. I had no key, and Mrs Flaherty often helped herself to a piece of candle or a knob or two of my coal.

She worked hard as a cleaner in two or three pubs, and she was soon asking me to keep an eye on Annie so that she could work evenings as well. I think she was addicted to the smell of alcohol. I reckon a match would have ignited a couple of inches from her mouth.

It wouldn't be fair to describe my room as a black hole of Calcutta, it was more of a dark greyish-brown. Walls, ceiling and floor merged indiscernibly into this colour, undisturbed by the rickety chest of drawers, small table, two chairs and narrow iron bed. Ugly as it was, it was a haven compared with the big brightly lit clean teashop in Oxford Street where I worked as a Nippy.

I was terrified by my job. There are good waitresses, they keep calm, there are bad waitresses, they keep calmer: 'Sod the cus-tomers, let 'em wait', and there are nervous, anxious-to-please hopelessly inefficient ones – I was one of the latter.

The working hours of the staff were staggered so that the maximum number were on duty during the rush hours, yet it was still grossly inadequate.

My five tables seated twenty diners. At twelve noon, from shop counters, offices, machine shops and the pavements, customers rushed in like the hordes of Babylon. They were always in a hurry. Sensible waitresses took the orders from one table at a time, ignoring the desperate tuggings at their skirt and the beseeching, urgent voices. They were cruel to be kind. I tried to be kind by taking twenty orders, so jumbled up by the time I reached the service counter that most of them were forgotten.

A great many of the items on the menu were pre-cooked at a central depot and kept hot or cold in a honeycomb of metal compartments along the counter. The counter hands filled them up from the back, the waitresses taking out their orders from the front. Often they were empty, as in the mad rush the four or five counter hands tried to cope with the myriad orders for this or that on toast which they had to prepare behind the counter, as well as mixing and dispensing all drinks, hot and cold.

The customers turned us into impatient despots, we turned the counter hands into wild-eyed viragos threatening to remove our entrails with the knives they brandished. Upstairs, in the steamy noisy bedlam of clattering crockery and cutlery, the washers-up screamed out invective about the ceaseless demand for clean replacements. It was like being on a treadmill in Hell. None of my customers ever actually had a seizure but some came near it.

We did not get much stamina from the food provided with the job. The staff took their lunches at half past ten or eleven o'clock. A tiny portion of tough red meat (I wonder if it was horse?), some greyish potato that had been put through a mincer to make it appear more palatable, and a small mound of worm-shaped rice pudding for afters of a quality even worse than Miss Lowry's – this was a typical meal. It cost us one-and-six a week. Two shillings a week were also deducted for our uniform, from our wages of thirty-one shillings. It took us six months to pay for, and we were immediately made to order another set. Then there was our insurance stamp, and it was automatically assumed we would contribute threepence a week to the employees' sports ground somewhere in the suburbs.

It was the firm's policy to place waitresses in a teashop a bus ride from their home address – this meant a couple of bob a week for fares. For tea, which was free, we got some bread and butter and a penny bun. The cups of tea that went with it were the best I've ever tasted.

If we worked in a teashop that closed late, on evening duty we were allowed threepence-ha'penny off the menu for our supper. We could augment this by buying extra at discount prices. Hunger made me a spendthrift. I often had only one pound left to pay my rent, coal and candles, off-duty food, black stockings for work, entertainment and saving up for holidays. 'You should be like me,' said one of the girls. 'I often earn myself ten shillings a time going out with some of the customers.'

Yet a good percentage of waitresses were cheerful, well-balanced girls.

My weekly day off frequently came on a Sunday. They were halcyon days. After his dinner, Syd called to take me out. I had always found London a place of wonder and interest, but I had only been looking at the casket; Syd showed me the jewels inside.

The museums – British, Science, Victoria and Albert, the National Gallery – treasure troves of exhibitions, free, or paid for with a pittance. He took me to the gods at Sadler's Wells. Syd had an innately cultured mind, and he had been to Grammar School. I followed in the wake of his deeper, richer appreciation. But he had desires of the flesh as well as the spirit – he wanted to take me to bed. He was barely twenty – I was two and a half years older.

I remembered a verse I had once read:

There was a young lady so wild
She kept herself pure undefiled
By thinking of Jesus
Venereal diseases
And the dangers of having a child.

I sensed the implied sneer, but I thought the young woman had a sensible idea of self-preservation.

I wasn't worried about Jesus. I was, however, concerned with my own self-respect, and very scared of getting pregnant. I was at the same time very curious about this mysterious world of sex. For many months Syd cajoled and sulked, while I kept up my defences.

One winter evening Syd took me for an unsuccessful swimming lesson. Seeing him so near to nakedness gave me courage – I gave in to his demand.

There was no light in my landlady's room – she had told me she was spending the night away. We sneaked upstairs – no need for a candle, enough light filtered through the window to undress by. Syd tactfully looked at the view while I got into bed. I squeezed up close to the wall and buried my burning face in the pillow. Syd had assured me he would take no risks. Presently he got in beside me – thin and bony though he was, it was very uncomfortable in the narrow bed. Fear, prudery, inexperience and above all the horrifying thought of Mrs Flaherty discovering us turned me into a cold, unresponsive object.

With no encouragement from me, Syd too lost his nerve. We were two failures together. We buried our faces in each other's necks like lost babes in the wood. But it was nice to have each other's company, holding hands in the dark.

Above my head my romantic dreams started floating away – the handsome desert sheik carrying me off from the tent where I was held prisoner, Clark Gable in the Edgware Road realising that the girl turning the corner into Molyneux Street was the very one he wanted for his next leading lady. These dreams dissolved for ever.

Now thirty-five years married, we know we found our way. It has been a most rewarding partnership. We started our own family tree, branching sturdily. We made our own dreams.